Hindle Wakes ('Hen-of-the-Wake')

GLADYS MANN

TRADITIONAL BRITISH

cooking for pleasure

PAUL HAMLYN · LONDON · NEW YORK · SYDNEY · TORONTO

Cover by courtesy of Whitbread and Company Limited

ILLUSTRATOR Rosemary Aldridge
DESIGNER   Jan Wiltshire

Published by
THE HAMLYN PUBLISHING GROUP LIMITED
LONDON · NEW YORK · SYDNEY · TORONTO
Hamlyn House, Feltham, Middlesex, England

First published 1967
Second impression 1969

Printed in Czechoslovakia by Polygrafia, Prague
T 2062

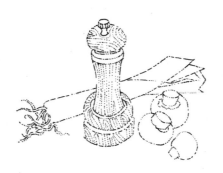

1587991

CONTENTS

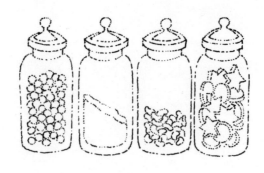

INTRODUCTION

Recently I was entertaining American friends at a restaurant, famous for traditional British fare, when one of them said, leaning back contentedly after his dinner of roast sirloin and Yorkshire pudding, 'I don't know why you Britishers are so modest, almost apologetic about your food. Why do you go crazy about Continental dishes, why do you try to imitate them and neglect your own? Look what you've got — the best of everything...' And he reeled off a list of foods for which Britain has been justly famous for centuries, right up to the 1914–18 war. Then before we had time to get back to our old standards, came the Second World War and after-war restrictions more severe than the war years. It is often said that no one under the age of fifty has had the opportunity of knowing and appreciating good British food.

We lost interest in food and cooking when there was nothing to cook; it became the rule of necessity to live out of tins to supplement meagre rations. Only if you lived in the country and turned your lawn into a vegetable patch, and kept your own hens and pigs and a cow, could you keep up anything like the standard of good eating to which we had been used.

But now we are back to normal; we can buy any food we want; it is our own fault if we do not learn again the joy of good eating in the British way.

That there is a trend back to traditional British food is shown from the growing demand for it in the better hotels and restaurants in London and in the more progressive provincial towns and villages. Old favourites are creeping back on to the menus, and customers, particularly businessmen and tourists from the Continent and America, are loving them. As well as the joints of prime meat, the steaks, chops, poultry and game, our excellent fish, plaice, haddock, halibut, salmon and trout, the homlier British country dishes are having a come-back. Boiled beef and carrots, pork and pease pudding, steak and kidney pudding, pork pie, pigeon pie, jugged hare, Lancashire hotpot, Irish stew, dumplings, English grill, jellied eels and cockles as well as oysters, all are being tried for the first time by many people and found to be just as enjoyable as Continental food eaten on holiday. Many people who consider themselves good judges of food say that British food is inclined to be stodgy and unimaginative. A famous chef has said that the distinction between French and English cuisine is that whereas French cooking is refined, British cooking is plain. But is that something to be ashamed of? Should we be apologetic because we are perhaps the only country in the world where calcannon, spotted dog, apple dumpling, steak and kidney pudding and pie, etc. are served? Let's be proud of our food and make a speciality of it; let's have our splendid puddings and pies, roasts and teabreads and scones. Come to that, there's no reason why we should be diffident about fish and chips, well sprinkled with coarse salt and vinegar. (We must grant that the French gave us chips.) I must warn visitors, though, not to expect really good fish and chips anywhere in London or the south. The best come from the heavy-woollen districts of the West Riding of Yorkshire. Apart from the careful selection and preparation of the fish — only haddock, cod, or skate for general sales, and plaice cooked specially if you want to be 'posh' — (none of the anonymous stuff that goes under the generic term of 'rock salmon' in the south), the secret of the characteristic deep brown colour and nutty taste lies in the frying medium. In the West Riding they use clarified beef dripping; other parts of the country use lard.

We have in Britain a rich store of local recipes and regional dishes, and it would be a good thing if every hotel or restaurant featured the dish peculiar to its town or county. Who wouldn't be curious to try, at least once, Cumberland Rum Nicky, or Bucks Bacon Badger, Maids of Honour or Lardy Cake if they read them in a menu?

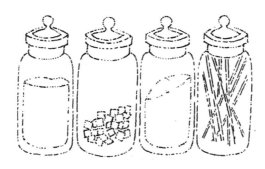

Which brings me to another of my pet grouses — menus printed in what is often mis-spelt or phoney French for every item no matter how British the dish. Oh yes, I know that French is the classic language of the culinary profession, and after all we should know enough French to be able to cope with a menu. Many of us have spent holidays in France and wrestled with menus there, but in our own country, why on earth should we give good, honest British foods French names? Snobbishness? — or just another sign of our inferiority complex about our own food and cooking? When I see an item such as Baron de Boeuf Rôti à l'Anglaise, Sauce Raifort, I begin to fume. What's wrong with Roast English Baron of Beef, Horseradish Sauce? It *is* English, isn't it?

I have been a collector of old or little-known recipes for a long time. The search for traditional British recipes is a fascinating one. Many family recipe books are hand-written and have been handed down from mother to daughter. There is a natural link between the kitchen and good cooking. The homes of a few generations ago often had what was known as a 'living kitchen', with dresser, large wooden table and chairs, an open range for cooking and heating, and a smaller 'working kitchen' and scullery which held the sink, where vegetables were prepared and the messier part of the preparation of food was done.

Interest in British home cooking began to drop, I think, with the coming of small kitchens. In the cubby-hole kitchen with scarcely room for more than one person, the housewife, unless she had a real love of cooking, soon became bored working on her own, so she did as little as possible.

True or not it is significant that the old idea of the family kitchen-dining room is coming back. The search for 'different' recipes has become a hobby. It is interesting to notice too, how the modern equivalent of old methods of cooking are returning. What is the latest rotary spit but an adaptation of the old rotating roasting jack or spit turning before the fire? Does the ghost of some long-ago 'spit-boy' ever look down at electrically turned spits and wonder, remembering the weary hours he spent turning the wheel of the carcass-laden spit in front of the roasting fire? And the barbecue, the modern recognition of the fact that you can only get real grilled meat by cooking it over the heat so that the fat spurts up and gives that superb charred outside to the meat, while keeping it tender inside? You should really have an open fire to do that, but many of our grill eating-houses today have adapted gas and electricity to use in the same way and get pretty nearly the same result. And cooking stoves, too, after the big turn over to gas and electric cooking, the solid fuel range is becoming popular again, and not least because it also heats the room with a solid, steady heat and always has an oven at the ready for slow cooking.

Pots and pans too: the old iron pans and cauldrons would not be given house room today, but enamel covered iron pans and casseroles are all in favour

for it has been discovered, as our forebears well knew, that an iron pot retains the heat better than anything else, and once hot, acts as a little oven in itself. Food cooked in an oven-to-table enamelled iron dish will keep hot throughout the meal. The old-fashioned brown stew jar or casserole, too, rubs shoulders with the finest modern kitchen gadgets on the shelves of the most 'with it' kitchen shops and boutiques.

WEIGHTS AND MEASURES

Weights throughout the book are given in lb. and oz. Capacity measure in Imperial pints and fractions thereof, with small amounts in spoon measures. For the benefit of American readers liquid ingredients have been given to the nearest U.S. standard cup measure. These follow the English measure i.e. 1 pint (U.S. 2½ cups).

All spoon measures refer to the British Standards Institution specification. All measures are levelled off to the rim of the spoon. To measure fractions of spoons use the small measures provided in measuring sets or divide the level spoon. The American standard measuring spoons are slightly smaller in capacity than the British standard measuring spoons. The proportion however is similar in that 3 American standard teaspoons equal 1 tablespoon.

HANDY CONVERSION TABLE
(Approximate conversion table)

ENGLISH MEASURE		AMERICAN CUPS
1 lb.	Butter or other fat	2 cups
1 lb.	Flour (sifted)	4 cups
1 lb.	Granulated or Castor Sugar	2¼ cups
1 lb.	Icing or Confectioners' Sugar	3½ cups
1 lb.	Brown (moist) Sugar	2¼ cups
1 lb.	Golden Syrup or Treacle	1⅓ cup
1 lb.	Rice	2¼–2½ cups
1 lb.	Dried Fruit (chopped)	2–2½ cups
1 lb.	Raw Chopped Meat (finely packed)	2 cups
1 lb.	Lentils or Split Peas	2 cups
1 lb.	Coffee (unground)	2½ cups
1 lb.	Dry Breadcrumbs	4 cups
8 oz.	Butter or Margarine	1 cup
8 oz.	Lard	1 cup
7 oz.	Castor Sugar	1 cup
7 oz.	Soft Brown Sugar	1 cup (packed)
7 oz.	Candied Fruit	1 cup
6⅓ oz.	Chopped Dates	1 cup
6 oz.	Chocolate Pieces	1 cup
5 oz.	Currants	1 cup
5½ oz.	Cooked Rice	1 cup
5¾ oz.	Seedless Raisins	1 cup
5 oz.	Candied Peel	1 cup
5 oz.	Chopped Mixed Nuts	1 cup

5 oz.	Sliced Apple	1 cup
4½ oz.	Icing Sugar	1 cup (sifted)
4 oz.	Cheddar Cheese	1 cup (grated)
3½ oz.	Cocoa	1 cup
2½ oz.	Desiccated Coconut	1 cup
2 oz.	Fresh Breadcrumbs	1 cup
1 oz.	Plain Dessert Chocolate	1 square
¼ oz.	Dried Yeast	1 packet
¼ oz.	Gelatine	1 tablespoon
¾ tablespoon	Gelatine	1 envelope
½ oz.	Flour	1 level tablespoon*
1 oz.	Flour	2 level tablespoons
1 oz.	Sugar	1 level tablespoon
½ oz.	Butter	1 level tablespoon smoothed off
1 oz.	Golden Syrup or Treacle	1 level tablespoon
1 oz.	Jam or Jelly	1 level tablespoon

* must be standard U.S. measuring tablespoon

METRIC EQUIVALENTS

It is difficult to convert to French measures with absolute accuracy, but 1 oz. is equal to approximately 30 grammes, 2 lb. 3 oz. to 1 kilogramme. For liquid measure, approximately 1¾ English pints may be regarded as equal to 1 litre; ½ pint to 3 decilitres (scant); 3½ fluid oz. to 1 decilitre.

OVEN TEMPERATURES

DESCRIPTION OF OVEN	APPROXIMATE TEMPERATURE CENTRE OF OVEN °F	THERMOSTAT SETTING
Very Slow or Very Cool	200–250	¼ = 240 ½ = 265 1 = 290
Slow or Cool	250–300	2 = 310
Very Moderate	300–350	3 = 335
Moderate	350–375	4 = 350
Moderately Hot to Hot	375–400	5 = 375 6 = 400
Hot to Very Hot	425–450	7 = 425
Very Hot	450–500	8 = 450 9 = 470

Note   THIS TABLE IS AN APPROXIMATE GUIDE ONLY. DIFFERENT MAKES OF COOKER VARY AND IF YOU ARE IN ANY DOUBT ABOUT THE SETTING IT IS AS WELL TO REFER TO THE MANUFACTURER'S TEMPERATURE CHART.

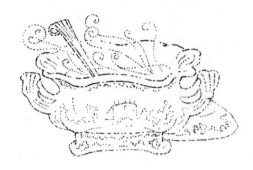

SOUPS AND FIRST COURSES

SOUPS

In the early days of the solid fuel kitchen range it was the obvious thing to have something simmering on the hob most of the day. In the stock pot or cauldron would be meat, vegetables, poultry and fish, in water well seasoned with herbs and spices — the meat was for the main course of a meal, and the liquor was served as a broth or soup, much as the French have always done with pot-au-feu. Any excess liquid would be kept to use as a foundation for sauces or other soups. Soup was almost incidental, a by-product; it was not common practise to buy special meats and bones especially to make it, nor was it prepared as a separate item or course.

Thus, mutton would be gently simmered in a large pot with vegetables and herbs, dumplings or plain suet pudding added, and all served as the main course, leaving behind the liquor. Next day, this was skimmed of all fat, some barley or dried peas or beans added (perhaps all three), root vegetables and any left over pieces of meat were put in, and the whole boiled and there was your soup or broth. The same with oxtail — only the smallest joints at the end of the tail were retained for the soup; the larger meaty pieces were served with vegetables as stewed oxtail.

In the same way, sheep's head, calves' head and ox head were used to form the basis of many dishes besides soup. Half an ox head (or 'beast's' head) would supply food in one form or another for a large family for the best part of a week: boiled with root vegetables, dried peas or beans and dumplings added later, along with the brains and scrappy pieces of meat, it made a fine broth. The tongue was served cold for high tea, while the ox cheek made the most delicious potted beef.

Other variations and combinations might be a ham shank or bacon knuckle boiled with pease pudding, for dinner and stock for pea soup; rabbits, hares and boiling fowls — the flesh for one meal and the innards left in the pot to make tomorrow's soup. Or a knuckle or shank end of veal would be boiled as usual with the vegetables but taken out before it got 'ragged', the meat removed from the bones and coated with a good cream sauce to appear as the meat course. A trick I use regularly when making white or jellied stock is to remove and chop up the meat and press it into a mould to provide jellied veal for high tea or supper.

It is somehow typical that Britain, the least soup conscious country, should choose for its traditional soup the most elaborate, expensive and difficult one to make. An ancient recipe for this starts off, 'Take a turtle weighing about 50 lb.'... Take it where? Not into any ordinary kitchen.

A rich mock turtle soup is good enough, the illusion of turtle meat coming from the gelatinous portion of calf's head.

It is interesting to know, too, that our much abused 'Brown Windsor Soup' was not invented by British Railways chefs or their predecessors but by a chef of Queen Victoria's, who created it as a nutritious broth for the young Queen when her first child was born in November, 1841. Obviously it achieved the name 'Windsor' on account of its royal connections but the chef did not call it that; it was named 'Calves Feet Soup à la Windsor' and was white in colour and rich and delicate in flavour. How then did it become *Brown* Windsor soup? How did a soup made from knuckle of veal, calves' feet, lean ham, chicken, vegetables and herbs with a dash of light white wine become brown, except by the addition of caramel? This is altering a classic recipe to suit some individual, which no self respecting chef would do. H. Smith (Master Recipes of Soups) gives 'Crème Windsor' — 'Prepare 3 pints (U.S. 7½ cups) cream of rice with rich veal stock. Add a sprinkling of thyme, garnish with calfs' feet, cut Julienne style (thin strips). Chopped hard-boiled eggs as garnish.' But M. A. Fairclough (Ideal Cookery Book) gives —

POTAGE À LA WINDSOR (WINDSOR SOUP)

8 oz. shin of beef, 1 carrot, 1 onion, 2 oz. butter, 2 oz. flour, 4 pints (U.S. 10 cups) stock, seasoning, 2 oz. boiled rice

Cut up the meat in small pieces, scrape the carrot, peel the onion, and slice them finely. Melt the butter in a saucepan, put the meat and vegetables into it and fry a nice brown. Add the flour, cook for a few minutes, then moisten it with the stock and stir until it boils. Simmer for 1 hour, then pass it through a fine sieve. Return to the saucepan and reheat. Season to taste with salt and pepper, add the boiled rice as a garnish and serve. Average cost 1/- (!), time required 1½ hours, seasonable at all times. Sufficient for 6 to 8 persons."

White or brown, the original Windsor soup seems a far cry from the unappetising brown paste concoction served today.

OLD ENGLISH OXTAIL SOUP

Preparation time   30 minutes
Cooking time   3 hours
To serve   4–5

You will need

1 medium-sized oxtail
4 pints (U.S. 10 cups) cold water
2 teaspoons salt
½ teaspoon black pepper
bunch of herbs
2 medium-sized turnips
2 onions
2 carrots
3–4 outer stalks celery

Have the oxtail cut into joints; remove surplus fat from root end.
Wash and dry the joints. Heat fat taken from root in a thick saucepan until liquid fat covers bottom of pan. Fry tail joints in this until all sides are sealed; remove them and put into large soup pan. Add water, salt, pepper and herbs, bring to the boil, skim, and simmer 2½ hours.
Fry diced vegetables in fat in which tail was fried, adding a little dripping if necessary, until well browned. Add these to soup pan and simmer until tender. Taste soup and adjust seasoning if necessary. Sprinkle with chopped parsley.
The large joints of oxtail are taken from the soup and served with vegetables as a meat course; the small pieces are served in the soup which may be thickened with a little flour mixed to a smooth paste with water.

Note

For a *very* rich brown, add a little beef bouillon, and for a real epicurean soup stir in two tablespoons of port wine or Burgundy just before serving.
The soup should be kept well skimmed of fat; it is really better to make it the day before required so that the solid fat can easily be removed when cold.

Old English oxtail soup

CREAM OF TOMATO SOUP

Preparation time 20–25 minutes
Cooking time 1 hour 20 minutes
To serve 4

You will need

1 lb. fully ripe tomatoes
1 oz. butter
6–8 bacon rinds
1 small carrot, sliced
1 small onion, chopped
2–3 stalks celery
1 pint (U.S. 2½ cups) white stock *or* water
½ teaspoon salt
¼ teaspoon white pepper
1 teaspoon sugar
2 teaspoons cornflour
¼ pint (U.S. ⅝ cup) top of milk *or* thin cream
few drops red colouring, if necessary
1 oz. butter, cut in 4 cubes

Slice the tomatoes; it makes sieving easier if they are skinned, but is not necessary. Heat butter, fry bacon rinds in it a minute or so, then add carrot, onion and celery. Fry without colouring 10 minutes. Add tomatoes and boil. Add stock or water, boil up and skim. Simmer for 1 hour. Pass soup through hair or nylon sieve. Reboil purée, adding salt, pepper and sugar. Blend cornflour to smooth paste with top milk or cream; add to boiling soup, bring

Cream of tomato soup

to boil, simmer 3 minutes. Add a few drops red colouring if necessary for brighter red. Serve in individual dishes or marmites with a cube of butter on top.

MOCK TURTLE SOUP

Preparation time 1½ hours
Cooking time 3 hours
To serve 5–6

You will need

½ calf's head
knuckle of veal, cut in three
5–6 pints (U.S. 12½–15 cups) stock *or* water
1 dessertspoon salt
4 oz. butter
2 large onions
4 cloves
4 outer stalks celery
1 medium-sized turnip
1 medium-sized carrot
bunch of herbs
6 peppercorns
rind half lemon
1 tablespoon cornflour
1 teaspoon mushroom ketchup
1 teaspoon anchovy essence
1 teaspoon lemon juice
2 tablespoons Madeira *or* brown sherry

Wash head in several waters, leave to soak in salted water for 1 hour. Wash the knuckle.
Put head and veal into large pan with the stock or water to well cover, add salt, and simmer 2–2½ hours, removing scum. Take up head and remove tongue and meat from bones; cut it into ½-inch cubes and leave to go cold. Melt butter in saucepan, fry onion, sliced, until browned. Put this into saucepan containing veal knuckle, calf's head bones and trimmings; add remaining onion stuck with the cloves, the chopped vegetables and herbs, peppercorns and lemon rind. Simmer 1 hour, strain through fine strainer. Return liquor to pan, boil up and add cornflour mixed to a smooth paste with a little water, simmer 3 minutes. Add pieces of meat and tongue from calf's head, ketchup, anchovy essence and lemon juice and simmer 10–15 minutes. Lastly add the Madeira or sherry.

SPLIT PEA SOUP

Preparation time about 20 minutes,
                    after peas soaked overnight
Cooking time   2–2½ hours
To serve   3–4

You will need

½ pint (U.S. 1¼ cups) dried split peas
2 pints (U.S. 5 cups) boiled bacon stock,
  or a few bacon bones in plain water
1 large onion
2 carrots
1 medium-sized turnip
1 outside stalk celery
½ oz. flour
salt if required, bacon will make water salty
¼ teaspoon pepper
onion rings, to garnish

Wash peas and soak overnight in water or stock.
Bring to the boil, putting in bacon bones if used.
Peel and chop vegetables, simmer in soup pan with
stock 1½–2 hours, according to the hardness of the
peas.
Remove bones and rub soup through a fine sieve.
Mix flour to smooth paste with some stock or
water and add to the purée.
Boil up and simmer 2–3 minutes. Taste, add salt
if required and the pepper. Serve, garnished with
onion rings.

Split pea soup

Susan's soup

Note

2 teaspoons chopped mint can be placed in the
tureen before pouring in the soup.

SUSAN'S SOUP

Preparation time 20 minutes
Cooking time   30 minutes
To serve   4

You will need

1 lb. potatoes, cut into sticks
2 onions, sliced
4 carrots, sliced
2 turnips, diced
3 oz. butter
2½ pints (U.S. 6¼ cups) water
salt and pepper
1 bay leaf
1½ oz. flour
¼ pint (U.S. ⅝ cup) milk
chopped parsley

Prepare the vegetables. Melt butter in a large pan
and sauté the vegetables.
Add water, seasoning and bay leaf and bring to
the boil. Cover and cook over a moderate heat for
25 minutes until all vegetables are tender.
Blend flour and milk together and add to the soup,
stirring. Cook for a minute and pour into a tureen.
Sprinkle with chopped parsley.

SCOTCH BROTH

Preparation time about 30 minutes
Cooking time 2½–3 hours
To serve 6

You will need

2 lb. shank *or* scrag end mutton
4 pints (U.S. 10 cups) water
2 carrots
2 turnips
2 outside stalks celery
3 leeks
2 oz. pearl barley
bunch herbs
1 teaspoon salt
½ teaspoon pepper
1 dessertspoon chopped parsley

Have the meat well chopped; remove surplus fat and wash meat well. Simmer for 2 hours in a large soup saucepan with the water after brining to the boil. Skim well. Cut the carrots, turnips and celery into dice, and the leeks into slices across; rinse the pearl barley in a sieve under running hot water. Add these and herbs, salt and pepper to the soup and simmer until vegetables are tender. Remove the herbs; add chopped parsley. Take up meat and bones, chop the meat into small pieces and return to broth.

Scotch broth

WELSH LEEK SOUP

Preparation time 20–30 minutes
Cooking time about 2 hours
To serve 4–5

You will need

2 lb. middle neck of mutton
2 pints (U.S. 5 cups) water
1 teaspoon salt
¼ teaspoon pepper
2 oz. pearl barley
1½–2 lb. potatoes
1 large leek
3 tablespoon chopped parsley

Have the meat well jointed; wash it and remove excess fat and skin. Bring it to the boil in a large saucepan with the water, salt and pepper, then add the barley, first rinsing it under boiling water, and simmer 1½–2 hours, until meat is tender. Add potatoes, whole or cut into large pieces, and the leeks, cut into rings. Simmer for a further 20–30 minutes. Strain and serve the pieces of meat and potatoes separately. Remove as much fat as possible from the broth; reheat it with the pieces of leek and the chopped parsley, and serve.

COCK-A-LEEKIE SOUP (SCOTTISH)

Preparation time 25 minutes
Cooking time 2–2¼ hours
To serve 6

You will need

1 boiling fowl
2 lb. knuckle of veal
5–6 pints (U.S. 12½–15 cups) cold water, to well cover meat
1 teaspoon salt
¼ teaspoon pepper
4 leeks
1 whole carrot
1 whole turnip
bunch herbs
2 cloves
2 oz. rice

Have the fowl trussed for boiling and the veal chopped into 3 pieces. Wipe fowl with a cloth wrung out in hot water; wash knuckle. Put into large saucepan with water, salt and pepper. Boil up and skim well. Add leeks, washed and cut up, carrot, turnip, herbs and cloves, simmer 1½ hours. Wash the rice and add to the soup; simmer another 20 minutes or until rice is tender, skimming during boiling. Remove carrot, turnip and herbs, take up chicken and knuckle of veal. Cut the chicken in half; reserve one half to be eaten cold or any other way, cut the meat from the other half in neat pieces and return to the soup. Reboil soup and pour into tureen.

QUEEN VICTORIA'S CHICKEN SOUP

Preparation time 30 minutes
Cooking time about 1½ hours
To serve 5–6

You will need

1 small young chicken
4 oz. lean bacon
1 onion
1 carrot
sprig of parsley, thyme, a bay leaf
1 teaspoon salt
¼ teaspoon white pepper
4 pints (U.S. 10 cups) white stock
 or vegetable water
4 oz. fine white breadcrumbs
¼ nutmeg, grated
1 oz. chopped almonds
½ pint (U.S. 1¼ cups) milk
¼ pint (U.S. ⅝ cup) thin cream

Have chicken trussed for boiling. Remove rind from bacon, cut into strips; peel and slice onion and carrot. Put bacon, vegetables and herbs in large stewpan, place chicken on top, sprinkle with salt and pepper, pour in stock. Cover closely and simmer until chicken is tender, about 1½ hours. Strain, returning liquor to stewpan. Remove meat from chicken, rejecting skin, pound the meat, adding the breadcrumbs and nutmeg until mixture is quite fine. Put in stewpan. While chicken is cooking, simmer the almonds in the milk until quite soft, rub through a grater. Just before serving, mix cream with almonds and add to the soup.

Queen Victoria's chicken soup

ENGLISH GARDEN PEA SOUP

Preparation time about 20 minutes,
 after shelling peas
Cooking time 30 minutes
To serve 3–4

You will need

1 lb. garden peas, after shelling
1½ pints (U.S. 3¾ cups) white stock
 or vegetable water
small bunch parsley sprigs
2 stalks fresh young mint
1 teaspoon granulated sugar
white parts 3 spring onions
2 oz. butter
½ oz. flour
½ pint (U.S. 1¼ cups) milk
½ teaspoon salt
¼ teaspoon white pepper

Reserve 3 tablespoons of peas, boil them separately in salted water. Add remaining peas to boiling stock or vegetable water, with the parsley, mint, sugar and spring onions. Boil until peas are soft, strain. Remove parsley, mint and onions; rub the peas through a fine sieve into the stock. Heat the butter in the soup saucepan, stir in the flour smoothly, then hot milk, stir until boiling. Add the sieved soup and bring it to the boil, simmer 2–3 minutes. Add salt and pepper and the peas cooked separately. Serve sprinkled with mint.

POTATO SOUP (IRISH)

Potato soup (Irish)

Preparation time 25–30 minutes
Cooking time about 1 hour
To serve 4–5

You will need

2 lb. potatoes
1 large onion
1 outer stalk celery
2 oz. butter
½ pint (U.S. 1¼ cups) milk
1½ pints (U.S. 3¾ cups) water
1 teaspoon salt
¼ teaspoon pepper
2 oz. fine sago
2 tablespoons thin cream
chopped parsley, to garnish

Potato soup (Irish)

Peel and cut up the potatoes and onion roughly; wash and cut up celery. Heat the butter in a saucepan and fry vegetables in it until all are coated with the butter, but not discoloured, about 5 minutes. Add milk, water, salt and pepper, boil gently 30–45 minutes. Remove celery and rub potatoes and onion through a sieve. Boil soup up again and add the sago, and let it simmer until sago becomes clear and thickens the soup. Remove pan from heat and add the cream; do not reboil after adding cream. Pour into soup tureen and sprinkle with chopped parsley. Serve with croûtons of fried bread.

FIRST COURSES

Fruits, such as grapefruit, melon and orange did not figure so much as they do today as first courses in traditional British meals. Unless the main course was something fishy, it was more in keeping with our natural resources to serve sea-food, shellfish or crustaceans.

There is little doubt that oysters, in season, are the most popular 'starters' for the British lunch or dinner and enjoy the longest tradition. In Britain, we have a fixed idea that the best oysters in the world come from our native waters, and having tried them in many countries I am bound to say that there is truth in the idea.

A whole book could be written about oysters. Oyster-beds are protected by stringent laws and tests, with special courts set up to manage them. In Colchester, in Essex, the Mayor and Corporation go out in full regalia to witness and sample the first catch of the season — for the best 'natives' come from Colchester, and from Whitstable in Kent.

What is a 'native'? Strictly speaking the term applies to oysters bred, reared and fattened in the same beds, as distinct from those that have been re-laid from one breeding ground to another for fattening. Compared with American and Continental oysters English natives may be small but their delicate, almost nutty flavour is to be found in no others. They have very small beards.

Because they are so tender and delicious, it is sacrilege to think of cooking English natives; that is a fate to be reserved for imported ones. Nor should they be spoilt by the addition of palate-ruining sauces and vinegars. A squeeze of lemon juice is permissible, and crisp celery is often served. Thin brown bread and butter is usually handed.

Fresh oysters should have tightly closed shells. Opening them is rather a knack. Insert a sharp pointed knife (there are special oyster knives) at the hinge and give a sharp twist. This severs the ligament which attaches the oyster to the flat shell, so that it drops into the deep shell, in which it is served with its own liquor, and nothing more.

A word of warning, don't drink spirits with oysters; stout, beer, ale or lager only are safe.

PRAWNS IN ASPIC

Preparation time 2 hours
Cooking time no cooking
To serve 6

You will need

1 pint (U.S. 2½ cups) aspic jelly, using aspic jelly
   crystals
12 oz. shelled prawns
4 oz. unshelled prawns
1 large lemon, sliced

Rinse out a 1½ pint mould with cold water. Pour
into it 3 tablespoons of liquid jelly, twist the bowl
round, in a bowl of ice if possible, until jelly coats
sides thinly. Leave jelly that runs down to the
bottom of the mould until it is on the point of
setting and arrange a layer of shelled prawns all
over it. Allow to set, then cover with a layer of
liquid jelly and another layer of prawns. When
this is on the point of setting put in the remaining
shelled prawns and fill up the mould with the cold
aspic on the point of setting. Allow aspic to seep
among the prawns and around sides of mould.
Leave until quite cold and set, then turn out on to
a shallow dish and garnish with lemon slices,
unshelled prawns and cress.

Prawns in aspic

PRAWN COCKTAIL WITH SOURED CREAM SAUCE

Divide 1 small shredded lettuce and 8 oz. shelled
prawns between 4 glasses.
Blend together 1 tablespoon tomato ketchup, dash
Worcestershire sauce, seasoning and 1 carton soured
cream.
Pour over lettuce and prawns. Sprinkle with paprika
pepper.
Garnish with whole prawns and lemon slices.
These are especially good served chilled. Serve
with thin brown bread and butter.

WHITEBAIT

Preparation time 15 minutes
Cooking time 4–5 minutes
To serve 4

You will need

1 lb. whitebait
2 oz. flour
½ teaspoon salt
¼ teaspoon pepper
lard for deep frying
cayenne *or* black pepper
lemon quarters
thin, buttered brown bread

The whitebait should be very fresh; wash them
and place in bowl with a few pieces of ice in it.
Mix flour, salt and pepper and put it on a clean
tea towel. Take up the ends of the towel and toss
fish in the flour until all are coated. Shake them
in a clean towel to remove surplus flour. Have
ready a pan of deep, hot lard; put the fish in the
frying basket and lower it carefully into the hot
fat and fry 3–4 minutes, keeping the basket moving
all the time. When crisp and very pale brown, lift
the basket, let the fat drip off, then empty whitebait
onto a piece of kitchen paper for a minute or so.
Put on to a hot dish and serve at once sprinkled
with cayenne or black papper and lemon quarters
for squeezing. This is usually served with buttered
brown bread.

PORK PÂTÉ

(Illustrated in colour on opposite page)

Preparation time 1 hour
Cooking time   1½–2 hours
To serve   5–6

You will need

1 lb. pig's liver
8 oz. belly pork
2 small shallots
4 tablespoons soft brown breadcrumbs
1 teaspoon salt
½ teaspoon black pepper
¼ teaspoon ground nutmeg
¼ teaspoon ground mace
1 large egg
1 tablespoon red wine *or* port

Wash liver, removing any skin or tubes; soak it for an hour in salted water. Cut two thin slices from pork and cut rest into small pieces discarding rind. Drain liver, cut it into medium-sized pieces; put liver and pork through a meat mincer twice, then pound it in a basin with the end of a wooden rolling pin, or in a pestle and mortar. Grate shallots and add to the liver and pork, mix well, then add breadcrumbs and seasonings and beat mixture well while adding beaten egg. Lastly add wine or port. Pack into a well-greased earthenware casserole, cut remaining two slices of pork into strips and arrange these criss-cross over the pâté. Cover with aluminium foil or oiled paper and lid of casserole.
Stand casserole in a tin with water to come about 3-inches up it and bake in a very moderate oven (335°F. or Gas Mark 3) for 1½–2 hours.
Leave to go quite cold and serve from casserole with thin buttered toast or water biscuits.

SALMON MOUSSE

(Illustrated in colour on opposite page)

Preparation time 1 hour
Cooking time   30 minutes
To serve   6

You will need

1 tail-end of salmon, 1½–2 lb.
1½ pints (U.S. 3¾ cups) water
2 tablespoons vinegar
6 peppercorns
1 teaspoon salt
8 oz. white breadcrumbs
1 oz. softened butter
1 egg yolk
1 tablespoon tarragon vinegar
2 tablespoons tomate purée
1 teaspoon black pepper
½ oz. powdered gelatine
2 tablespoons hot water
1 egg white
mayonnaise, cucumber, parsley and hard-boiled
   egg, to garnish

Wrap salmon in muslin and boil it in water, vinegar, peppercorns and salt for 25–30 minutes until tender. Take up, remove skin and bones and put the flesh in large bowl. Mash it with a fork. Add breadcrumbs, softened butter and beat well. Stir in egg yolk, add tarragon vinegar, tomato purée, pepper and beat with a wooden spoon until quite smooth. Dissolve gelatine in hot water and stir into the mixture; whip egg white until stiff and fold in. Pack the mousse into an oiled, fish-shaped or plain mould pressing it well down. Cover with greaseproof paper or foil and leave in a cold place for 3 hours or until set. Turn out onto a serving dish and just before serving, garnish with piping of mayonnaise and sliced cucumber, parsley and hard-boiled egg.

Salmon mousse; pork pâté; tomato salad; Melton Mowbray pie; pressed brisket of beef

Roast loin of pork and apple rings

MEAT

I believe it is as true today as ever it was that there is no meat in the world so good as the British; if you doubt it, take a look at the beasts at Smithfield Show — the biggest beauty show on earth, with the Queen as chief judge of the Herefords and Aberdeen Angus.

So it is surprising that with such naturally good material to start with, the end product in restaurants and hotels is so often disappointing. The justly famous 'Roast Beef of Old England' at its juiciest and best has to be looked for, but it is a worthwhile search.

So far as British home cooking is concerned, the primary cause of frustration, failure and disappointment is lack of knowledge in buying meat. During the meat starved years of rationing this became a lost art, with the result that many young housewives tell me that they dread going to the butcher because they don't know what to ask for. In those days we just had to take a 'piece' tied up with string, its origin quite unrecognisable, instead of asking for a joint by name. The art has never been regained, yet if a housewife could insist on the butcher cutting a particular joint she wants, or at least see it on the bone, she would get a more satisfactory roast.

What we call roast meat today is really baked meat; *roasting* was done in front of an open fire with roasting jack and screen. The method is still unbeatable, for the steady turning of the jack browns and cooks the meat evenly in front of the radiant heat, and there is little shrinkage and a wonderful flavour.

The earlier method, roasting on the spit, was more suitable for larger joints and even whole animals. The meat was impaled on a rod resting on 'dogs' before the fire, and had to be turned more or less constantly to get even roasting. The spit is turned mechanically today when this method is used, as in some good hotels, to roast birds, sucking pigs and other small animals. Indeed, electrically operated rotisserie spits for home use are becoming very popular.

Oven roasted meat should be cooked in an open tin in a hot oven, so that it comes into contact with dry heat on all sides to get the characteristic brown 'crust'. In a covered roasting tin steam forms and keep the outer meat moist. Only tougher joints, requiring long, moist cooking should be cooked in the covered tin, and even then the cover should be removed towards the end of cooking to allow the meat to get a good brown outside.

BEEF

The lean of prime beef should be a deep red colour, firm yet springy to the touch and marbled with fat; the fatty part should be creamy coloured, although this can vary according to the breed and diet of the beast. Avoid pinky-coloured beef: this is a sign that the meat has not been well hung and will be tough and flavourless.

The method of cutting up beef into joints varies in different parts of the country.

The London cut is the most generally accepted one of which the others are usually deviations or splittings up. In America the cuts are different again.

The prime joints for roasting are:

SIRLOIN — best and most expensive. Try to get a little of the undercut with it which is sometimes removed and sold with the fillet. There should be a nice, not too thick border of fat on the outside and a creamy piece of fat underneath. To get the best out of sirloin the joint should have three short ribs and never less than two; the weight of course depends on the size of the beast. A 4—5 lb. joint is advisable for really good flavour. Cold sirloin is almost as good as hot, though the undercut should always be served hot; it is sliced separately so that everyone gets a share.

Failing an open fire or rotisserie for roasting, the joint should be placed upright in a roasting tin with a little dripping in the tin to start the roasting. Put it in a hot oven (425°F. or Gas Mark 7) until the outside is sealed, 10—15 minutes, then reduce heat to moderately hot (375°F. or Gas Mark 5) for the rest of the cooking time, allowing 15 minutes to the pound; baste often during cooking. Sirloin should always be underdone. Serve with traditional Yorkshire pudding, see page 94, horseradish sauce, page 149, mustard and clear gravy.

WING RIBS — these come next to the sirloin and are treated in the same way. A minimum for a good standing joint is 2 ribs; serve with the same accompaniments as sirloin.

(Illustrated in colour on the jacket)

WING RIBS AND LONG RIBS — these are continuations of the wing ribs, cut with longer rib bones. Many people like them boned and rolled as they find them rather ungainly on the bone. A better and more economical way, I think, is to have the piece with the thin end bones sawn off to cook separately.

AITCH BONE — is the joint over the rump, very good but a bit ungainly in shape; it can be braised or roasted. It is often called 'poor man's sirloin' as the meat is similar in quality but much cheaper than sirloin.

TOPSIDE — a very lean solid cut, usually a piece of fat is tied to the side to help in the roasting. It must be roasted slowly and basted carefully otherwise it will be hard and tasteless. A covered tin is useful, really pot-roasting is better.

BOILED BEEF, CARROTS AND DUMPLINGS

Preparation time 25 minutes, including vegetables and dumplings
Cooking time 1 hour 50 minutes
To serve 5—6

You will need

3 lb. salt silverside
1 large onion
1 lb. carrots

FOR THE DUMPLINGS

4 oz. flour
1 level teaspoon baking powder
2 oz. shredded suet
¼ teaspoon salt

Soak meat several hours in cold water. Rinse and put into large pan with cold water to just cover. Bring to boiling point, remove scum, add onion, peeled and chopped roughly. Cover tightly and simmer 1 hour. Then add peeled and quartered carrots and simmer 30 minutes longer.

TO MAKE THE DUMPLINGS

Mix all dry ingredients, add cold water slowly to make a pliable dough. Form into small balls, about the size of a golf ball, on a floured board, add to

Boiled beef, carrots and dumplings

pan and boil 20–25 minutes. The dumplings will swell to about twice their original size, so do not make them too big. Dish up meat on to hot dish, lift out carrots and dumplings with a perforated spoon and put them round the meat; serve a little of the liquor in a gravy boat. The remaining liquor is an excellent stock for soup. Extra onions may be put in the pan at the time of adding the carrots; the original one will have disappeared by the time the meat is done.

PLANKED STEAK

Preparation time 10 minutes, including potatoes
Cooking time 15–20 minutes
To serve 4

You will need

1½–1¾ lb. rump *or* fillet steak
1 bay leaf
small bunch herbs
mashed *or* duchesse potatoes, see page 63
little butter, salt and pepper
chopped parsley

There is a belief among the American that the Planked Steak is an American idea but long before the Pilgrim Fathers left these shores to sail to America, meat was baked on a plank; and no doubt they kept up the custom. In the old days the plank was oak, about 18-inches square, the centre hollowed out a little. The plank was rubbed all over with suet or dripping, and heated in an oven or before the fire. In the hollow was placed herbs and clove of garlic and hot dripping. The steak was laid over this, given a coating of dripping and the plank placed in a very hot oven. The meat was turned once, but after that the oven door was not opened again until meat was cooked. The wood burnt a little, giving the meat a slightly smoky taste, and in the hollow would be a delicious aromatic gravy. Nowadays, planks with grooves and a channel around the edges for catching the juices, can be bought. The steak is lightly grilled first, then placed on the well greased plank, sprinkled with herbs, salt and pepper and dotted with butter, a border of mashed potatoes put all round. The plank is put in a hot oven (425°F. or Gas Mark 7) until meat is done and potatoes lightly browned, 12–15 minutes. The steak and potatoes are sprinkled with chopped parsley.

Stewed steak and kidney

STEWED STEAK AND KIDNEY

Preparation time 20–25 minutes
Cooking time 2½–2¾ hours
To serve 4–6

You will need

1½ lb. stewing steak
8 oz. ox kidney
2 large carrots, sliced
1 large onion, sliced
2 oz. dripping
1 oz. flour
1½ pints (U.S. 3¾ cups) stock *or* water
1 level teaspoon salt
¼ teaspoon pepper
parsley, to garnish

Wipe the beef, cut into smallish pieces, removing surplus fat or skin. Remove fatty core and skin from kidney; cut into small pieces. Heat fat in frying pan and fry meat lightly in it; remove to stew pan. Add carrots and onion. Sprinkle the flour in the fat left in frying pan, stir until smooth; cook until flour is browned. Stir in stock or water, add pepper and salt, stir until boiling. Pour into stew pan. Place over low heat and simmer for 2–2½ hours. Pour into serving dish; garnish with parsley and extra carrots.
It is traditional to serve dumplings (see page 22) with stewed steak and kidney. Add them 20–25 minutes before the meat is cooked.

ENGLISH GRILL

Preparation time 25 minutes
Cooking time 12–15 minutes
To serve 4

You will need

1½–2 lb. rump or fillet steak, in 4 pieces
melted dripping, oil or butter
black pepper from pepper mill
½ teaspoon coarse salt
4 large tomatoes
8 medium-sized mushrooms
salt and pepper

CRISP FRIED ONIONS

4 large onions
little milk
1 tablespoon salted flour
deep fat for frying

PARSLEY BUTTER

2 oz. butter
1 teaspoon chopped parsley
squeeze lemon juice

Ideally, steak should be grilled *over* a hot clear red fire, so that, as the meat cooks, spurts of fat drop into the fire and flare up, giving the slightly charred taste characteristic of grilled steak. Nowadays, it is more often done *under* the griller. It is important that the outside should be quickly sealed first, so that no juices escape. Griller should be red hot; rack in grill pan should be greased. Have steak cut 1 to 1½-inches thick. If bought in the piece, cut it into portions for serving before grilling. Brush steak all over both sides with melted dripping, oil or butter, sprinkle with ground pepper and coarse salt. Place meat on rack in grill pan, around it arrange tomatoes, halved and sprinkled with salt and pepper and coated with dripping, and in the bottom of pan put cleaned mushrooms, also sprinkled with salt and pepper; they will cook in the drippings from the steak. Place grill pan under red hot grill near the heat, for a few minutes, then turn the steak with tongs or between two spoons; never a fork.
Grill a few minutes on second side, turn steak again and finish grilling first side; turn and finish grilling second side. An under-done or rare steak should not take more than 12 minutes in all; after this you can vary time from 12–15 minutes for medium or well done. The steak should be a dark rusty brown outside and inside red and running with juice — real gravy. When steak is done the tomatoes and mushrooms will be ready. Serve on hot dish or straight on to plates and pour mushroom flavoured juices from grill pan over the steaks; place a square of parsley butter on top of each.

CRISP FRIED ONIONS

Peel onions, cut into thin slices, separate slices into rings. Put in a basin, cover with milk. Put salted flour on a towel; heat fat in a deep pan. Drain the onion rings in colander, then toss them in flour; shake in dry towel to remove excess. Put onions in frying basket, lower carefully into hot fat; fry a minute or so, then lift basket, let fat get really hot again and submerge basket a second time, until onions are golden and crisp. Lift up basket, let fat drip off. Drain on absorbent paper, then pile on hot dish and serve at once.

TO MAKE PARSLEY BUTTER

Chill butter in a small basin, work in chopped parsley and few drops lemon juice. Form into oblong and place in fridge to firm up; cut into four when ready to serve steak.

BEEF ROLLS OR OLIVES

Preparation time 30 minutes
Cooking time 1¾ hours
To serve 4

You will need

1½ lb. lean beef, cut in thin slices, topside
  or toprump are good
6 oz. forcement, see below
2 oz. dripping
1 onion
1 outside stick celery
1 small carrot
salt and pepper
1 oz. flour
1 pint (U.S. 2½ cups) stock *or* water
1 tablespoon mushroom ketchup
3 cloves

FOR THE FORCEMEAT

4 oz. breadcrumbs
2 oz. shredded suet
2 teaspoons chopped parsley
½ teaspoon mixed herbs

½ teaspoon salt
¼ teaspoon pepper
1 onion, finely chopped
grated rind of ½ lemon
1 small egg
little milk *or* stock, if necessary

Cut meat into neat pieces, about 4-inches square. Beat with rolling pin or steak bat until they are about 2-inches longer than wide. Spread thinly with forcemeat, roll up and tie.

Heat dripping in a thick saucepan or flameproof casserole and fry the olives for a few minutes until lightly browned all over. Take up and keep hot. Chop vegetables and fry lightly in the same fat, sprinkling with salt and pepper. Add flour and cook and stir until a pale brown. Pour in stock and ketchup and add cloves. Return beef olives to pan, cover with greased paper or aluminium foil and tight fitting lid, and simmer for 1½ hours. Remove string from olives; arrange them on hot dish. Strain and season sauce and pour over.

Beef rolls or olives

TO MAKE THE FORCEMEAT

Mix all dry ingredients and onion and lemon; bind stiffly with beaten egg and milk or stock if necessary.

LAMB AND MUTTON

There is nothing more delicious for dinner than English or Scotch lamb, especially in early summer when garden peas are about and there is plenty of fresh mint for mint sauce.

The flavour of lamb and mutton vary a lot according to where the animals where reared. Downland lamb and mutton, particularly Southdown, is sought after by epicures, being very tender, though not so lean as the sweetfleshed mountain sheep. Lamb and mint 'go' together, traditionally, but it's just as natural to use other herbs in cooking it. After all, lambs and sheep eat the wild herbs, thyme, sage, rosemary, marjoram, along with the grass when they can (Welsh mountain sheep, for instance) and some people claim to detect a distinct flavour of herbs in such meat. Be that as it may, a sprig of rosemary, or a sprinkling of mixed herbs over the fat of lamb does add wonderful flavour.

IRISH STEW

Preparation time 25–30 minutes
Cooking time 2 hours
To serve 4–6

You will need

2 lb. middle neck of lamb
1 lb. onions, sliced
3 lb. potatoes, sliced
1 teaspoon salt
¼ teaspoon pepper
1½–2 pints (U.S. 3¾–5 cups) stock *or* water
chopped parsley, to garnish

Chop meat into neat pieces, rejecting surplus fat. Sprinkle meat, onions and potatoes with salt and pepper. Put a good layer of potatoes in saucepan, on top put alternate layers of meat, onions and half remaining potatoes. Add stock or water to just reach the top of meat, etc., cover and simmer for 1½ hours. Arrange remaining potatoes neatly on top, they should not lie in gravy, cover so they cook in steam for 30–45 minutes. Serve meat on a dish; arrange potatoes from top around it; the potatoes in the bottom will have absorbed a lot of fat from meat and may be unpalatable, but where economy is important they are often served as well. Sprinkle with chopped parsley.

CROWN ROAST OF LAMB WITH MUSHROOM STUFFING

Preparation time   1 hour
                     (allowing for making crown)
                     30 minutes without making
                     crown
Cooking time   2½–3 hours, according to weight
To serve   8

You will need

2 pieces best end of neck, 7 cutlets each, 3¾–4 lb.
a little dripping
mushroom stuffing, see below

FOR THE STUFFING

12 oz. mushrooms
2 oz. butter
3 tablespoons chopped celery
1 small onion, chopped
1 tablespoon chopped parsley
12 oz. white breadcrumbs
1 teaspoon salt
¼ teaspoon pepper

The butcher will usually make the crown for you though he may charge a little extra for doing this. If you care to try the job yourself, ask the butcher to chine the meat that is, cut off the thick back bones so that the joints can be easily shaped into a ring.
Cut the meat from the end bones for a distance of about 4-inches, scraping the bones quite clean; make short cuts between the bones at the thick end so joints bend easily. Now tie the two joints together in a ring with the bones on the outside. Using a trussing needle (a thick darning needle or carpet needle can be used) and thin twine, join the two pieces of meat together at top and bottom. Tie string round the middle. Pack pieces of meat cut from the end bones inside the crown. Fill up with stuffing. Now weight it.
Clean the mushrooms, cut into small pieces. Heat butter and toss mushrooms in it for 5 minutes. Take them out, and in remaining fat fry celery, onion and parsley until the onion turns yellow. Stir in the breadcrumbs, add mushrooms, salt and pepper and mix all ingredients thoroughly.
To roast, stand the crown in baking dish with a very little dripping to start roasting. Cover end bones with a strip of greaseproof paper or aluminium foil to prevent charring. Cover stuffing with paper. Place in hot oven (450°F. or Gas Mark 8) for

Crown roast of lamb with mushroom stuffing

25–30 minutes. Reduce heat to moderately hot (375°F. or Gas Mark 5) and continue cooking allowing 20 minutes to the lb. plus 20 minutes. Remove paper from end bones and put cutlet frill on each. Serve with carrots and peas and duchesse potatoes, see page 63. Put a few slices of carrot on top of stuffing. It is quite easy to carve the crown.
Remove the string, and holding the joint firm with the carving fork inside, divide the cutlets by slipping the carving knife down between each bone. Two cutlets should be allowed for each serving with some of the stuffing.
Crown roast is particularly delicious served cold, the meat being extra juicy and full of flavour through being cooked gently so no juices escape from the centre.

LAMB CASSEROLE

Preparation time   20 minutes
Cooking time   2½ hours
To serve   4

You will need

2 lb. scrag *or* middle neck
1½ lb. potatoes
1 oz. dripping
8 oz. onions, sliced
1 oz. flour
1 pint (U.S. 2½ cups) stock *or* water
salt and pepper

Lamb casserole

Cut meat into pieces, removing excess fat. Prepare and cut potatoes into chunks. Brown meat in the dripping. Add onions and fry lightly. Remove meat and onions, and stir in flour. Cook for a few minutes. Add stock or water and bring to boil. Put a layer of potatoes in casserole with meat and onions. Season each layer with salt and pepper. Pour on the gravy; top with a layer of potato chunks. Cover with a lid and cook in a moderate oven (350°F. or Gas Mark 4) for 2½ hours. Half an hour before the end of cooking time, remove the lid to allow the potatoes to brown.

ROAST SADDLE OF LAMB

Preparation time 15 minutes,
                    after preparation by butcher
Cooking time 3½–4 hours, according to weight
To serve   12–14

You will need

1 whole saddle lamb, approximately 10 lb.
2 teaspoons mixed herbs, thyme, parsley,
    marjoram, mint
½ teaspoon powdered mace
1 tablespoon flour
1 teaspoon salt
½ teaspoon pepper
2 sprigs rosemary
a little dripping

The butcher shortens the rib bones to 3-inches from the backbone, taking out the ends of the rib bones. It is traditional to roast joint with the tail on. The two kidneys can be left in the meat, or removed and roasted alongside the meat, encased in their own fat. The latter is the better way, as in carving the joint a slice of the kidney should be given with each serving, and it will be easier for the carver if he doesn't have to search for them inside the joint.

The thin flaps along the undersides of the saddle are cut off and surplus fat removed. The sides are then folded under, the whole skin removed and joint tied securely in shape. It's traditional to slip sprigs of rosemary under centre trussing string.

Mix herbs, mace, flour, salt and pepper and sprinkle all over prepared joint. Cover with greaseproof paper spread with dripping, then with foil and place in a baking tin with ¼ pint (U.S. ⅝ cup) hot water added. Put in the kidney. Cook in hot oven (425°F. or Gas Mark 7), for 15 minutes, then reduce heat to moderate (350°F. or Gas Mark 4), allowing 20 minutes to the pound plus 20 minutes. Baste 3 or 4 times during roasting; 20 minutes before the end, remove paper and foil, increase heat to hot (425°F. or Gas Mark 7) return meat to oven for top to crisp and brown. Dish up on to hot dish; remove trussing strings. Take off fat from kidneys, place on dish for serving. Keep hot while making gravy.

TO MAKE GRAVY

Carefully strain off fat from roasting tin, leaving sediment. Place tin over low heat, sprinkle a tablespoon of flour into sediment, stir until smooth. Add ¾ pint (U.S. 1⅞ cups) stock slowly, stirring until boiling, simmer 2–3 minutes. If gravy is not a good colour it is permissable to add a little gravy colouring, nothing is so unappetising as greyish brown lamb gravy. Taste and season gravy as required, then strain into hot sauceboat.

NOTE ON CARVING

Saddle of lamb is carved along the backbone in long slices from neck to tail end. The slices should not be too thick, this is the prime part of the joint and if cut too thick there may not be enough to go round. Each long slice should be cut into two or three pieces. With each serving of this prime meat, a small portion of crisp fat and meat from the underside and a slice of kidney should be served. Serve with mint sauce, see page 149, and red currant jelly.

Lancashire hot-pot

LANCASHIRE HOT-POT

Preparation time 20–30 minutes
Cooking time 1¾–2 hours
To serve 6

You will need

2 lb. best end neck of lamb cut into 6 chops
2 lb. potatoes, peeled and sliced
salt and pepper
pinch powdered nutmeg and mace
3 lambs' kidneys
1 large onion, sliced
6 oysters
½ pint (U.S. 1¼ cups) lamb stock, made from
   trimmings from lamb
little butter

Wipe the chops, remove excess fat and skin. Grease a casserole put a layer of potatoes in the bottom, then arrange the cutlets on top. Season with salt and pepper, nutmeg and mace. Place sliced kidneys and onions on top, add the oysters, and cover with a thick layer of potatoes. Pour hot stock into the dish, down the side, season with salt and pepper. Brush the top with melted butter, cover with a buttered paper and cook in moderate oven (350°F. or Gas Mark 4) for 1¼ hours. Remove paper and continue baking a further 25–30 minutes longer until top is crisp and brown.

Note

Traditional Lancashire hot-pot was made in a tall brown earthenware stew jar so that chops could stand on end with half a kidney between each, and one oyster to each chop.

Oysters were cheaper then; they may be omitted. But with or without oysters Lancashire hot-pot was far from being the makeshift dish many people think it.

GRILLED GIGOT CHOPS

Preparation time 15 minutes, including sauce
Cooking time 20 minutes
To serve 4

You will need

4 gigot lamb chops, *Scottish chops cut from the leg*
salt and pepper
2 tablespoons cooking oil
parsley
8 oz. green gooseberries
½ pint (U.S. 1¼ cups) water
½ oz. butter
1 tablespoon sugar
grated rind ½ lemon
pinch mixed cake spice
1 teaspoon chopped mint

Prepare, and if necessary, trim the chops. Brush the bars of the grill pan with oil and heat grill. Brush chops over with oil, then season with salt

Grilled gigot chops

and pepper. Place chops under hot grill, turning them over after 2–3 minutes to grill the other side. Reduce heat and continue cooking about 15 minutes, turning the chops from time to time. Arrange the chops on an ashet; garnish with parsley; serve with gooseberry sauce.

TO MAKE SAUCE

Top and tail gooseberries; stew in the water until soft. Beat well, then rub through hair or nylon sieve. Return to pan, beat in butter and sugar and reheat. Add lemon rind, spice and mint.

PORK

There was a time in Britain when most country dwellers (and suburban dwellers) who had a back yard or garden, kept their own pigs. The pig was often the family's main meat supply. When the pigs were killed there was a wonderful source of fresh meat for pork joints, pork pies, puddings and brawn, salted and cured meats, hams and bacons, lard for pastry, bread and cakes, enough to last from Autumn to Spring. It can truthfully be said of the pig 'Nothing is wasted but the squeak'.

Then a law was passed forbidding pig keeping near the house, and pig keeping became strictly for country people. A lot of good things became expensive or impossible to obtain for town dwellers. At one time it was considered unwise to eat pork unless there was an 'R' in the month, the Winter months. But modern pig farming, hygenic feeding and housing, have made it quite safe to eat pork all the year round.

Pork should *always* be well cooked; when judging the time for cooking allow for thickness and the shape of the joint.

ROAST LOIN OF PORK AND APPLE RINGS

(Illustrated in colour on page 20)

Preparation time   30 minutes
Cooking time   1 hour 40 minutes
To serve   6

You will need

3½–4 lb. loin of pork
little olive oil
1 lb. cooking apples
1 small can whole cranberries

FOR THE SWEET AND SAVOURY SAUCE

¼ pint (U.S. 1¼ cups) stock *or* hot water
½ pint (U.S. 1¼ cups) stock, from roasting tin
1 tablespoon canned cranberries
1 tablespoon tarragon vinegar
2 teaspoons Demerara sugar
1 tablespoon tomato ketchup
1 heaped teaspoon cornflour
1 tablespoon cold water

Choose a piece of pork with the kidney in if possible; this improves the flavour. Have the meat chined by the butcher, and the rind well scored. Do not wash the meat but wipe it with a cloth wrung out in hot water. Place meat in roasting tin and grid and brush the rind with olive oil. Cover with waxed paper or foil and place in centre of pre-heated very hot oven (450°F. or Gas Mark 8). When the meat has cooked for 1 hour, remove the paper or foil, brush the rind again with olive oil, and cook for a further 30–40 minutes uncovered, to allow the rind to become crisp.

Fifteen minutes before meat is done, wash apples, do not peel them, core and slice them and place them in the fat in roasting tin, then cook until lightly browned.

Put meat on a hot dish and place the apple rings around joint. Reserve one tablespoon of cranberries for the sauce, garnish apple rings with remaining cranberries.

Pour off the fat left in the meat tin and add ½ pint (U.S. 1¼ cups) hot water or stock to the tin, stir well to mix in the brown sediment and use this stock as basis for the sauce.

TO MAKE THE SAUCE

Put stock into saucepan, sieve cranberries, add to stock, bring to the boil, add vinegar, sugar and ketchup and stir over low heat until sugar dissolves. Blend cornflour to a smooth paste with the cold water, add to sauce in pan and stir until boiling. Simmer for 2–3 minutes until sauce clears and thickens slightly. Pour into sauceboat.

BOAR'S HEAD

The preparation of a boar's head is not a job to be undertaken unless you have infinite patience and a certain amount of skill with the boning knife. Traditionally a wild boar's head should be used, but since the hunting of the wild boar has long since gone out of fashion, a full-grown pig's head must suffice. And a very good substitute it is too, if not too big.

Some old recipes say that the head should be boned before it is cooked, and the cavities filled with small pieces of meat, so that the original shape is carefully preserved, but I do not advise a novice to do this. The boning can be done after boiling, and it requires little skill to mould the meat into its proper shape with the help of string and skewers. Have the head cleaned and split in two by the butcher; there should be a little flesh and skin left unsevered at the top. The snout and eyes are removed and discarded; the ears are removed but will be used, and the brains should be kept separate as they cook, quicker than the rest of the head. Let head lay under running water for an hour or so. Then rub it well with coarse salt and leave in a bath of salted water overnight. Make a mixture of 1 lb. coarse salt, 1 oz. saltpetre, ¼ oz. black pepper, 1 grated nutmeg, ¼ oz. mustard seeds, ¼ oz. powdered mace. Rub mixture all over head, after draining it from water. Lay it in a large bowl and turn it daily, rubbing the pickle well in, for 5 or 6 days. Take it up and drain, and put it on to boil with some root vegetables, a bunch of sage, a few bay leaves and peppercorns. Boil until the bones are dropping out. Add brains, tied in muslin, 20 minutes before head is done; ears require about an hour's

boiling. Let head cool in the broth, then take it up and remove bones, disturbing the flesh as little as possible. Skin the tongue, put it back; replace the brains as near as possible to their proper position. Put the two halves of head together, working the flesh into a conical shape, and tie with tapes. Flatten head slightly under a weight, and leave to go cold. Remove ears from broth and leave to go cold.

TO MAKE GLAZE

Boil broth rapidly to reduce it, adding bones and trimmings from head, egg shells and a little vinegar and gravy browning. When the glaze is beginning to set, brush it over the head, placed on a dish. Fasten ears to the head with small skewers, and glaze them. Glaze head several times, allowing it to become quite set between each application. The last layer of glaze should be poured over to give a smooth finish.

Now the head can be decorated as you wish with pipings of lard, black olives surrounded with egg white for eyes, pieces of bone for tusks and the dish garnished with apples, quartered hard-boiled eggs etc. The head will keep for several days, and is best carved downwards from the back.

FAGGOTS (SAVOURY DUCKS)

Preparation time 15–20 minutes
Cooking time 40–45 minutes
To serve 4–5

You will need

1 lb. pig's liver
4 oz. pork fat
1 large onion
1 teaspoon mixed herbs
nutmeg to taste
salt and pepper
8–12 oz. breadcrumbs
pig's caul

Chop liver and fat finely; chop onion into dice. Put in pan with herbs, cover closely and cook gently for 30 minutes, without browning.

Drain off fat, cool mixture slightly, then add nutmeg and seasoning to taste and sufficient bread-crumbs to make a fairly stiff mixture. Cut the caul into 4-inch squares, put a square piece of the mixture in centre of each, and fold the caul around it, making square parcels. Place in a baking tin with a little gravy and brown quickly in hot oven (425°F. or Gas Mark 7). Serve with rich, thick brown gravy.

Note

A more popular North country way is to pack the prepared faggot meat in a Yorkshire pudding tin, mark it into squares, cover it with the caul and bake in the hot oven (425°F. or Gas Mark 7). Known as 'Ducks with veil on'. Pig's fry is often used instead of just pig's liver.

PORK BRIDIE (SCOTTISH)

Preparation time 25–30 minutes
Cooking time 35 minutes
To serve 4–6

You will need

10 oz. short pastry, see page 77

FOR THE FILLING

12 oz. shoulder pork
6 oz. turnips *or* swedes
4 oz. onions
2 oz. lard
salt and pepper
1 egg, beaten

Roll out pastry into a large circle, about 12-inches. Cut the pork very finely and add the chopped turnips or swedes and onions. Fry in lard for about

Pork bridie (Scottish)

10 minutes. Season well with salt and pepper and allow to cool. Place this filling in the centre of one half of the pastry circle. Brush edges, fold over other half, and seal. Crimp edges, brush with beaten egg and bake in moderately hot oven (400°F. or Gas Mark 6) for approximately 35 minutes. Serve hot with vegetables or cold with salad.

BOILED PORK AND PEASE PUDDING

Preparation time 20–25 minutes
Cooking time 1¾–2 hours
To serve 4–6

You will need

3 lb. salt pork, hand *or* belly
2–3 sage leaves
6 peppercorns
3 medium-sized parsnips
1 carrot
1 onion
small piece turnip
1 stick celery
1 small firm cabbage

FOR THE PUDDING

1 pint (U.S. 2½ cups) green split peas, soaked overnight
salt and pepper
mint
1 oz. margarine
1 egg

Place meat in a large saucepan, cover with warm water, bring to the boil, skim, boil for 15 minutes, then add sage, peppercorns and vegetables all cut up coarsely. Half an hour before meat is done, add quartered cabbage.

TO MAKE THE PUDDING

Tie the split peas in a cloth with a sprig of mint and seasoning. Tie securely, but allow room for peas to swell. Suspend bag in pan with boiling pork and boil for 1 hour. Take out, and rub peas through coarse sieve, mix in margarine and egg, season again with salt and pepper, replace in clean cloth and boil with the pork again for a further 30 minutes. Lift out pudding, unroll it from its cloth onto a hot dish. Pull it apart with forks to serve; do not cut it. Serve with the pork, vegetables and some of the pork stock.

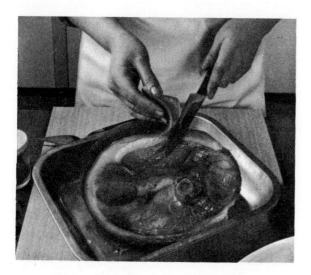

BRITISH HAMS AND BACON

The curing of the flesh of the pig was one of the oldest domestic crafts in Britain; no countrywoman would think of being without one or two home cured hams to 'cut at' throughout the year.

The methods of curing, which varied with each locality, were closely guarded secrets. All sorts of homely herbs and flavourings were used; some used dry salting and some brine salting. Even the drying, or smoking of hams differed. The simplest way was to hang the hams in the inglenook or from hooks in the kitchen ceiling, leaving them to cure in the smoke from the domestic fire, no matter what kind of wood was burning. Smoke from resinous wood, such as pine, was supposed to give a dark, fly proof finish. Oak chips were considered the best for giving a mild smoky flavour. It is said that the original York hams were smoked with the oak sawdust collected during the building of York Minster.

TO BOIL A HAM

Wash the ham in several waters and leave to soak for 24 hours. Wipe dry and remove the rust, the brown part of the underside left by the salting and curing. Put a layer of chopped vegetables in a large saucepan or fish kettle, onions, celery, carrots and turnip, add a bunch of herbs, a dozen or so peppercorns, put in the ham, pour over it 1 pint (U.S. 2½ cups) rough cider and 1 lb. West Indian treacle and around it arrange 6 or 8 unpeeled apples each stuck with 2 cloves. Pour in water to cover the ham and leave to simmer 4 to 5 hours. Leave to go cold in the liquor, take up the ham, remove the rind and sprinkle with raspings. Or the fat can be sprinkled with brown sugar and stuck with cloves, and glazed before a clear fire or in the oven, if yours is big enough.

TO BAKE A HAM

After the ham has been boiled and the skin removed, slash the fat, marking it in squares or diamonds. In each square or diamond place a clove. Stand the ham in the roasting tin and sprinkle brown sugar over. Pour ½ pint (U.S. 1¼ cups) cider in the tin, place in hot oven (425 °F. or Gas Mark 7) and bake until the fat is well glazed basting once or twice with the hot cider.

BOILED BACON AND BROAD BEANS

This is a typical British meal when broad beans are in season. The beans should be young, before the outer skins have had time to toughen. Boil green or smoked bacon allowing 20 minutes to the lb. until 15 minutes before serving time, then add the shelled beans and simmer until done. Take up the bacon, skin it; strain the beans from the liquor and serve in a separate dish. Parsley sauce, see page 148, is the usual accompaniment to this dish.

HAM BAKED IN A CRUST

The crust can be what was known as 'common crust' that is, a paste of flour and water just the minimum of fat such as dripping or suet to help bind it, or it can be the basic suet crust, see page 78, as used for dumplings.

A whole ham, or gammon, which usually weighs anything from 11–14 lb. may seem rather big for modern families, but it is possible to buy half gammon or half a ham; or a fore-hock of bacon weighing 5–6 lb. is very cheap and suitable for this method.

In any case, the joint should be soaked at least 12 hours, longer if it is likely to be very salty. Cover meat all over with fairly thick common crust, making sure that joins are well sealed. Then wrap it in greased greaseproof paper. Stand it on a trivet in a roasting tin; put one inch of water in the tin. Place tin in hot oven (425°F. or Gas Mark 7) for 10 minutes, then reduce heat to moderate (350°F. or Gas Mark 4) and bake for 4 hours longer, for a 10 lb. joint, replacing the paper as it becomes burnt. (Modern aluminium foil can be used, and will not need replacing.) To serve, take up the gammon or ham, break off the crust as neatly as possible. Remove skin and sprinkle with raspings and garnish knuckle with a paper frill.

COLLAR BACON WITH PINEAPPLE

Preparation time 2–3 hours, for soaking
Cooking time 1 hour 40 minutes
To serve 8

You will need

4 lb. cut of collar bacon
1 small can pineapple slices
2 dozen cloves
1 level teaspoon mustard
4 oz. brown sugar

Soak the joint for 2–3 hours. Place in a pan of cold water, bring to the boil and simmer for 1 hour. Remove from pan and strip off the rind. With a sharp knife, score the fat criss-cross. Decorate with rows of small segments of pineapple, each secured with a clove. In a small saucepan, mix together mustard, brown sugar and pineapple juice. Place bacon in a baking tin and over it pour the sauce. Bake in a moderately hot oven (400°F. or Gas Mark 6) for 40 minutes, basting occasionally with the sauce.

Serve garnished with sprigs of parsley and with buttered potatoes and peas.

BOILED BACON WITH OATMEAL DUMPLINGS (SCOTTISH)

Preparation time 10–15 minutes
Cooking time 2–2¼ hours
To serve 8

You will need

4 lb. boned rolled forehock bacon
1 bay leaf
6 peppercorns

FOR THE DUMPLINGS

8 oz. self-raising flour
2 oz. fine oatmeal
3 oz. suet
salt and pepper
milk to mix

Soak the bacon 2 hours if unsmoked, 4 hours if smoked, rinse and put in a saucepan with the bay leaf and peppercorns. Just cover with cold water and bring to the boil. Reduce heat and simmer for 1¼ hours. Remove joint and strip skin off. Sprinkle with a little oatmeal.

TO MAKE DUMPLINGS

Mix flour, oatmeal and suet together. Season well. Mix into a stiff dough with the milk. Make into little balls and cook in the bacon liquid for 15 minutes. Serve the hot bacon cut in slices with caper sauce, see page 148, with dumplings and carrots.

Collar bacon with pineapple

Grilled gammon rashers

GRILLED GAMMON RASHERS

Preparation time 20 minutes, after soaking
Cooking time 10–15 minutes
To serve 4–5

You will need

4–5 gammon rashers, ½-inch thick
2 oz. melted butter
1 oz. cloves
8 oz. tomatoes
parsley, to garnish

Soak rashers in cold water for 30 minutes; dry them well. Remove rinds and brown edges. Make snips with scissors through the fat, about ½-inch apart. Brush one side of the rashers with melted butter; brush grid in grill pan with butter, then lay on the rashers buttered side uppermost and put under red hot grill for 4 minutes. Turn the rashers over, brush second side with butter, and push a clove in each cut section of fat. Put back under grill for 3–4 minutes; lower heat and grill for 3 minutes longer.

Slice tomatoes; spread them with melted butter. Place on the grid when turning rashers to second side; they will be done by the time the rashers are done.

Arrange rashers on hot dish with tomatoes alongside. Garnish with parsley sprigs. New potatoes can be served either on the dish or in separate dish; toss them in butter after boiling and sprinkle with chopped parsley.

BACON AND EGGS

Is there any dish more typically British than bacon, fried or grilled, with fried egg and fried bread for breakfast?

Back, streaky, collar or gammon rashers are all suitable for frying or grilling. Except for gammon, bacon is usually sliced thinly. Unless bacon is very lean, no extra fat is needed for cooking it. Before cooking, cut off rinds and rusty edges of bacon. Snip the fat about ½-inch downwards at intervals, to keep the rashers flat during cooking. If frying, place them in pan with the lean part overlapping the fat; so that the fat is in direct contact with the hot pan and prevents the lean sticking.

To grill bacon, place it on the rack in the grill pan, but in this case allow the fat to overlay the lean, since the heat will be coming from above directly on to the fat. Turn two or three times, until bacon is crisp to your liking. It is easier to get crisp bacon by grilling it, as the bacon does not lie in the fat.

For fried eggs, break each into a cup and slide carefully into the hot bacon fat. Cook until egg white sets, and baste to cook the yolk. Fried bread should be cooked after eggs, as it will use up all the fat. Stale bread is better for frying. Put medium-thick, small slices in hot fat, leave to absorb some of the fat, then turn and cook until crisp on the second side; turn back to first side and allow it to brown.

VEAL

Veal is not typically traditional British meat; it was never very popular among working people in the country. In fact, it was rather suspect, what was wrong with the calf that it had to be killed?

However, animals are now reared with the intention of killing them young and veal has become a popular meat. Much of it is imported.

Veal is apt to be insipid and always needs a good forcemeat cooked with it; as it is lacking in fat it is often combined with ham or bacon in cooking.

Fricassée of veal with bacon rolls

FRICASSÉE OF VEAL WITH BACON ROLLS

Preparation time 30 minutes
Cooking time 1½ hours
To serve 4

You will need

12 oz. cooking veal, sliced
1 medium-sized onion, peeled and stuck with
  2 cloves
1 bay leaf
1 dessertspoon salt

FOR THE SAUCE

2 oz. cooking fat
4 oz. mushrooms, peeled and sliced
2 oz. plain flour
¾ pint (U.S. 1⅞ cups) milk and veal stock
seasoning
2 tablespoons thin cream, optional

FOR GARNISH

8 rashers streaky bacon, rolled
fat for deep frying
2 slices crustless bread, cut in triangles
chopped parsley, to garnish

Put the prepared veal in a fairly large saucepan with the onion, bay leaf and salt. Cover with water. Bring to the boil, cover and simmer for 1–1½ hours. When cooked remove the onion and bay leaf.

TO MAKE SAUCE

Melt the fat in a fairly large saucepan. Add prepared mushrooms and fry gently for 2 minutes.

Remove a few for garnish and keep warm. Stir in the flour and cook for a further 3 minutes. Remove the saucepan from the heat and gradually blend in the milk and veal stock. Return the saucepan to the heat; stirring all the time, bring to boil and boil for 2 minutes. Add seasoning and cream (if used).

TO MAKE BACON ROLLS AND GARNISH

Skewer the bacon rolls. Brush with melted fat and place under hot grill for 2 minutes, turning occasionally. Heat fat in a pan to 360 °F. (or until a cube of day old bread turns golden brown in 1 minute). Fry the triangles of bread until a light golden brown. Remove and drain on crumpled tissue paper. Add the cooked veal to the sauce and reheat. Place in a warmed serving dish, garnish with bacon rolls, mushrooms and chopped parsley. Place triangles of fried bread around the edge.

CALF'S LIVER AND BACON

Calf's liver is considered the tenderest and best flavoured of all livers; it is certainly the most expensive. Calf's liver and bacon is classed as a dish for the epicure, served as a main course, too good to be treated as a mere breakfast dish. Fry the bacon rashers, remove and keep warm. Dust liver slices and a few onion rings with flour and fry very briefly in the bacon fat. Arrange on a serving dish and serve with gravy.

Calf's liver and bacon

FRIED CALF'S SWEETBREADS

Preparation time 40 minutes, including soaking
Cooking time 45 minutes
To serve 2–3

You will need

1 calf's sweetbread
1 pint (U.S. 2½ cups) white stock
salt and pepper
1 egg
fine breadcrumbs
butter *or* lard for frying

Soak the sweetbread in salted water ½ hour, rinse it and put in saucepan with cold water, bring slowly to the boil, boil for a minute or so, then strain through a colander and rinse under running cold water. This is known as blanching and must be done to the sweetbreads whatever way they are finally cooked.

Put them in a saucepan with the stock, season with salt and pepper, and simmer gently 20–30 minutes. Strain and press between two plates until cold, then cut into slices, dip in beaten egg, coat with breadcrumbs and fry in butter or lard, until crisp and brown. Drain well on kitchen paper.

Fried sweetbreads go well with bacon and can be fried in bacon fat.

ROAST VEAL

Veal should always be roasted slowly, with a generous amount of fat in the roasting tin. The top of the meat should be covered with fat bacon, or larded with fat bacon, and it should be frequently basted.

If the joint is unstuffed forcemeat balls should be placed in the tin to cook 30–40 minutes before the meat is finished. Allow 20 minutes to the lb. plus 20 minutes for thin cuts such as loin, best end of neck, blade or oyster, end of the shoulder, and 25 minutes plus 25 minutes for the leg, fillet end. Serve veal with thick brown gravy.

STUFFED ESCALLOP OF VEAL

Preparation time 25–30 minutes
Cooking time 20 minutes
To serve 4–5

You will need

2 lb. fillet of veal, sliced
salt and pepper
lemon juice
veal forcemeat, see below
4 oz. bacon
1 egg
breadcrumbs
2–3 oz. butter *or* cooking fat

Have the meat cut very thinly. Flatten it with a knife blade. Cut into strips about 4-inches long and 2-inches wide. Season with salt and pepper and a few drops of lemon juice. Cover with strips of thin bacon then spread with forcemeat. Roll up and tie. Coat with egg and breadcrumbs and fry gently in butter or fat turning frequently until well browned all over, 15–20 minutes. Place on a hot dish and serve with brown sauce, see page 148.

VEAL FORCEMEAT

Preparation time 10 minutes
Cooking time according to meat stuffed
To serve 4

You will need

4 oz. fresh white breadcrumbs
2 oz. shredded suet
1 tablespoon finely chopped parsley
½ teaspoon mixed herbs
grated rind ½ lemon
pinch powdered mace
salt and pepper
1 egg
little milk *or* stock

Mix all the dry ingredients together, bind with beaten egg and a little milk or stock, if necessary.

Beef steak and kidney pudding

Roast turkey

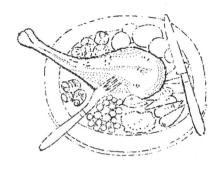

POULTRY AND GAME

CHICKEN

The hen is the oldest domestic bird in Britain; at one time every countrywoman (and many towns-women with a back garden) kept a few hens and a cockerel, to supply the family with eggs and the occasional chicken for the table, selling the surplus for 'pin' money; for the chicken and egg money was recognised as her 'perks'. Even on the farm, the chickens and eggs were the special care of the farmer's wife. For townspeople the supply of chickens was a limited and seasonal one, and therefore they were expensive and regarded as a special treat. But thanks to modern methods of rearing, housing and storage, chickens are an all-the-year round food and relatively cheap. The birds are killed while young; this means that although they are tender they are not as tasty as older birds. Oven ready birds can be bought from the grocer, the fishmonger and the supermarket as well as at the butchers' and the poulterer's. If you have time to shop around there is no doubt that free range chickens are better for flavour and as for 'oven ready', well, your butcher or poulterer will always get it ready for you, and truss it or cut it up as you want it. A very handy thing are the wrapped chicken portions for the small family or a special dish where a whole chicken is not needed.

The bird not always easy to come by every day is the boiling fowl; you'll probably have to order it a day or two in advance. But it makes one of the most economical and well-flavoured meals there is.

In the days when it was considered uneconomical to kill chickens before they were well grown, roasting was the chief British way of cooking them. But now that chickens are reared in a wholesale fashion you can buy them as young as you like for grilling, frying or casseroling. The fried chicken dinner is as popular in Britain as it is in America, while the spit roasted chicken, a near relative of the traditional jack roasted chicken, is one of the treats made possible by the modern rotissiere grill. Chicken for frying or grilling *must* be young and tender, as this is a quick method aimed to give a crisp, golden outer crust with tender, flavoursome meat inside.

It helps to know the type of bird to ask for. Thus, baby chickens (poussins) weighing from ¾–1½ lb. can be split in halves and are the most delicious for grilling; the flesh is so tender that they are cooked 'in no time at all'.

Spring chickens come next, known as poulets, and they are usually cut into four or six pieces for frying; they weight from 2½–3½ lb. Over that weight, up to 4½ lb., we get full grown fowls (pou-lardes) requiring the longer processes of cooking, roasting or casseroling. Older birds, over 4½ lb. are boiling fowls, but they can be casseroled whole or in joints. Capon is a male chicken castrated when young to increase its weight quickly and improve flavour. They grow as large as old cockerels but the flesh remains tender, and they can be roasted. They can be killed at least three days before they are dressed for cooking.

HINDLE WAKES (HEN-OF-THE-WAKE)

(Illustrated in colour on the frontispiece)

This is an old North Country dish, which used to be served for high tea during Wakes (holiday) week. It is a traditional way of serving a large, really old boiling fowl; the method of stuffing has changed little down the years. The boiling fowl was allowed to hang several days before cooking. The method of cooking was to boil overnight in a large pot and allow to cool in the broth. For a version of Hindle Wakes more suitable to the modern cooker, a capon can be used, and it is better to oven steam it. Being more tender than a boiler, it does not need the overnight cooking.

Preparation time	1 hour
Cooking time	4½–5 hours
To serve	8–10

You will need

1 large capon, 7–8 lb.
1 lb. stale loaf
1 lb. large prunes
4 oz. shredded suet
2 large teaspoons mixed herbs, thyme, sage, parsley, marjoram
1 teaspoon salt
½ teaspoon pepper
1 tablespoon soft brown sugar
prune juice and vinegar, half and half to make stiff mixture

Break bread up roughly and soak it ½ hour in cold water to just cover; wash and soak prunes overnight in water, drain them, but reserve the water. Squeeze excess water, if any, from the bread; crush bread with a fork. Chop prunes removing stones. Add prunes to bread, with as many of the prune stone kernels as you have patience to crack, mix well, then add the suet, herbs salt and pepper and sugar. Make a fairly stiff mixture with vinegar and prune juice, only a little will be required. Pack the stuffing into the neck end of capon, pressing it into a nice round shape. Secure the skin under the wing tips of the bird, using a small skewer, or by sewing it. Fill the body of the bird with remaining stuffing, pushing it well in. If there is not quite enough stuffing to well fill the body, pack a few prunes, whole, in the cavity. Close the vent securely,

it is best to stitch it with coarse thread, so stuffing will not leak during cooking.

Place bird on grid in deep roasting casserole. Cover breast thickly with dripping or cooking fat, then with a piece of wet muslin. Cover this entirely with a sheet of aluminium foil; the bird must be covered on all sides, but not underneath. Pour boiling water into the tin to just reach the bird. Place in a hot oven heated to (445°F. or Gas Mark 8) and immediately reduce heat to very moderate (335°F. or Gas Mark 3) and cook for 4–4½ hours, replacing water with more *boiling* water as the first evaporates. Leave to go cold in oven. Take up on to large serving dish remove trussing strings and skewers. Coat with lemon sauce, see below, and garnish with soaked prunes cut into slices, and lemon slices. Cold boiled ham, in slices, or wrapped around prunes usually accompanies this noble dish.

LEMON SAUCE

Preparation time	20 minutes
Cooking time	15 minutes
To serve	8–10

You will need

yellow rind and juice of 1 large lemon
½ pint (U.S. 1¼ cups) chicken stock
½ pint (U.S. 1¼ cups) milk
2 oz. butter
1 oz. flour
salt and pepper
½ oz. gelatine dissolved in 2 tablespoons hot stock
1 tablespoon thin cream
1 teaspoon grated lemon rind

Simmer lemon rind in stock and milk for 5 minutes. In another saucepan melt butter, stir in flour until smooth, then strain in lemon flavoured milk and stock. Stir over low heat until boiling; simmer 3 minutes. Remove from heat, season to taste with salt and pepper, and stir in the lemon juice, then add the dissolved gelatine. Lastly add the cream and the grated lemon rind. Allow sauce to cool, but not stiffen, before pouring over the bird. It is better to do this in two stages, first spooning the sauce in a thin layer over the bird and leaving to set. Then pour remaining sauce, in one go all over the bird so that it settles smoothly.

Roast chicken with sage stuffing

Shallow fried chicken

ROAST CHICKEN WITH SAGE STUFFING

Preparation time 20 minutes
Cooking time 1½ hours
To serve 3

You will need

1 oven ready chicken, 2½ lb. in weight

STUFFING

1 oz. best quality margarine
2 small onions, finely chopped
3 oz. fresh breadcrumbs
2 level teaspoons chopped parsley
½–1 level teaspoon dried sage
salt and pepper to taste
1 egg, well beaten
approximately 3 oz. fat *or* dripping for roasting
bacon rolls and sausages
watercress, to garnish, optional

Pre-heat the oven to hot (400°F. or Gas Mark 6). Remove the giblets from the chicken, and simmer the giblets in a little water to make stock for the gravy.

TO MAKE STUFFING

Melt the margarine in a frying pan, add the onions and cook gently until tender, about 5 minutes. Remove from the heat and mix in the crumbs, herbs and seasoning and finally sir in the beaten egg. Stuff the chicken and then place it, breast side down, in a roasting tin with the melted

dripping, and baste well. Cook for 1¼–1½ hours, turning the chicken onto its back for the last half of the cooking time, and basting once or twice. Serve hot with bacon rolls, sausages and gravy. Garnish with watercress.

SHALLOW FRIED CHICKEN

Preparation time 15 minutes
Cooking time 20 minutes
To serve 4

You will need

4 chicken joints
1 egg, well beaten
2 oz. fine breadcrumbs
½ teaspoon salt
¼ teaspoon pepper
pure vegetable oil for shallow frying

Wipe and dry pieces of chicken. Brush over with beaten egg. Mix breadcrumbs with salt and pepper on a sheet of paper; toss joints in them. Shake to remove surplus. Heat ½–1-inch of oil in thick frying pan; test with cube of bread. Place chicken in pan, starting with the leg pieces, skin sides down; do not overcrowd the pan. Fry until golden brown, turn pieces with two spoons or cooking tongs. (Avoid piercing coating and skin.) Fry 15–20 minutes turning again. Take up to drain on absorbent paper, arrange on hot dish and garnish with sprigs of watercress.

TURKEY

The turkey, compared with the hen, is a fairly new resident in Britain. Contrary to common belief it is not the oldest British Christmas bird; the goose is much more traditional. Remember the Cratchit Christmas dinner in Dicken's 'Christmas Carol'? 'There never was such a goose ... the youngest Cratchits in particular were steeped in sage and onions to the eyebrows'!

America can claim the turkey for her own, where it is a 'must' for Thanksgiving Day in November; it was introduced to Britain by the Spaniards, after the discovery of America. The best turkeys come from Norfolk and due to modern rearing methods are available all the year round.

ROAST TURKEY

(Illustrated in colour on page 38)

Preparation time 1 hour
Cooking time 5½–6 hours
To serve 8–10 (hot)

You will need

11–12 lb. turkey, drawn and trussed for roasting
6 oz. streaky bacon
  or 6 oz. cooking fat

FOR THE CHESTNUT STUFFING

1 lb. chestnuts
¼ pint (U.S. ⅝ cup) milk
¼ pint (U.S. ⅝ cup) stock
4 oz. streaky bacon
4 tablespoons white breadcrumbs
½ teaspoon mixed herbs
grated rind of 1 lemon
½ teaspoon salt
¼ teaspoon black pepper

FOR THE LIVER FORCEMEAT

1 lb. dry breadcrumbs
4 oz. shredded suet
1 medium-sized onion, chopped
cooked liver of turkey
1 dessertspoon chopped parsley
1 teaspoon mixed herbs
grated rind 1 lemon
1 level teaspoon salt
¼ teaspoon black pepper
giblet stock to bind

Wipe the drawn and trussed bird inside with a cloth wrung out in hot water. Sprinkle inside with salt. Loosen skin at the crop (neck) end, if this has been secured under the wing tips in trussing. Put the giblets in a pan with water to well cover, add large onion chopped roughly, a teaspoon salt, ½ teaspoon pepper and a sprig of parsley, thyme and sage, bring to the boil, skim and simmer for 1–1½ hours or until liver is tender.

TO MAKE CHESTNUT STUFFING

Wash chestnuts, slit the skins, boil nuts in water to well cover for 15 minutes. Take up a few at a time with perforated spoon, remove outer and inner skins while still hot, keeping rest of nuts hot in the meantime. (Skins tighten on again if allowed to go cold.) Stew skinned nuts in milk and stock 10–15 minutes. Strain, reserving liquid. Put nuts through meat mincer, or crush with fork. Cut bacon into strips; fry until crisp. Add bacon and fat extracted from it to the nuts, add breadcrumbs, herbs, lemon rind, salt and pepper, bind stiffly with milk and stock from boiling chestnuts. Pack stuffing into crop of bird, pressing it into a smooth, rounded shape; secure flap of neck skin with wing tips under body. If necessary secure further with a skewer.

TO MAKE LIVER FORCEMEAT

Mix breadcrumbs, suet and onion. Crush liver until crumbly, add to breadcrumbs, etc. with parsley, herbs, lemon rind, salt and pepper, mix well and bind stiffly with stock. Pack into body of bird, not too tightly as breadcrumbs swell. Push tail of bird over the opening, and tie ends of drumsticks securely behind. If the skin around the tail end is torn, or very loose, secure it by stitching with coarse thread, or with small skewers.

THE ROASTING

Cover the breast with streaky bacon or spread thickly with fat. Wrap it in double thickness of greaseproof paper or aluminium foil. Place in well greased roasting tin and put in middle of pre-heated oven to (310°F. or Gas Mark 2) and allow 25 minutes to the pound, so a 13 lb. bird (weight after stuffing) will take 5¼ hours. Remove foil 30 minutes before end of cooking time to allow the bird to brown.

Serve with cranberry sauce and giblet gravy, see opposite. Garnish with sprigs of watercress.

GRAVY

1 small onion
1 medium-sized carrot
6-inch piece celery
2 oz. lard or dripping
1 tablespoon flour
1 pint (U.S. 2½ cups) giblet stock

½ teaspoon salt
¼ teaspoon pepper

Chop vegetables, heat fat and fry these until lightly browned. Add flour, stir over low heat until smooth, add stock slowly, stir all the time until boiling again. Cover and simmer 10 minutes, then strain into sauceboat. A small glass sherry added just before serving is an improvement.

DUCK

Norfolk for turkeys, Aylesbury for ducks. Aylesbury ducks are known the world over for their flavour and meatiness. Though originally the name meant that the bird had been reared in Aylesbury, Buckinghamshire, this is not necessarily the case today, for breeding birds from the original stock have been sent all over Britain and the world. Certainly if you buy Aylesbury duck in this country you can be pretty sure that it sprang from Aylesbury stock and will be the best.

ROAST DUCK WITH ORANGE SAUCE

(Illustrated in colour on page 47)

Preparation time 40 minutes
Cooking time 1 hour 40 minutes
To serve 4

You will need

1 duck, 5 lb.
½ oz. flour
½ pint (U.S. 1¼ cups)
4 oranges
sage stuffing, see page 41

FOR SAUCE

1 orange
¼ pint (U.S. ⅝ cup) water
pinch salt
½ pint (U.S. 1¼ cups) stock
1 teaspoon cornflour
1 glass sherry, optional

Put the duck giblets in a pan with 2 pints (U.S. 5 cups) water with salt and pepper and a roughly cut up onion, and boil to make stock.
Pack the stuffing into the neck end of the duck and secure the flap of skin under the bird with a skewer. Place the duck on a grid in the roasting tin; prick the breast in several places, and around the leg joints. Cover with aluminium foil or grease-proof paper and roast in a moderately hot oven (400°F. or Gas Mark 6) for 1 hour. Remove the covering, prick the breast again and sprinkle with the flour. Return to oven, uncovered for a further 20–30 minutes.
Peel the 4 oranges and cut them into fairly thick slices across the sections, removing the pips. Put the slices in the roasting tin around the duck for the last 15 minutes of roasting. Dish up with orange slices around the duck, and garnish the dish with sprigs of watercress.

TO MAKE GRAVY

Pour off excess fat from roasting tin, add ¼–½ pint (U.S. ⅝–1¼ cups) stock to the residue, and boil up over low heat, scraping the brown pieces from sides and bottom of tin, to make gravy. Season with salt and pepper.

TO MAKE THE SAUCE

Cut off the yellow part of the orange with a sharp knife and cut it into match-like strips about 1-inch long, with scissors. Put these on to boil with water and pinch of salt until tender, about 10 minutes. Squeeze the juice from the orange and add it to the stock. Strain orange strips when tender and add to the orange juice and stock. Bring to the boil. Blend cornflour to a smooth paste with a little of the water used to boil the orange peel and add this to the boiling sauce. Stir over low heat until sauce boils and thickens slightly. Add the sherry (if used) and pour the sauce into sauce boat.

ROAST GOOSE, SAGE AND ONION STUFFING, APPLE SAUCE

For a medium-sized bird you will require four times the quantity of stuffing as for roast chicken see page 41, made in the same way. Pack into the body of the bird, after removing surplus fat from inside. Put into baking tin, breast side up. Being a fat bird, a goose is not spread with fat or bacon or covered with greased paper; instead, the breast is pricked near the legs and wings to allow the over rich fat to run out in cooking. A damp piece of muslin is placed over the breast. Roast in a hot oven (425°F. or Gas Mark 7) for an hour, then remove muslin, reduce heat and finish cooking. Three-quarters of an hour before the bird is done, baste the breast, sprinkle with flour and return to oven to brown.

Serve with apple sauce, see page 149, and thick brown gravy, made as for duck.

GAME BIRDS

The most traditional game birds in Britain are grouse, pheasant, partridge, pigeons; of these the grouse is considered the best, not only in Britain, but the world over. They are an excellent alternative to poultry for Christmas. It is usual to allow one young grouse per person.

ROAST PHEASANT

Preparation time 20 minutes
Cooking time 50 minutes–1 hour
To serve 4–5

You will need

1 brace pheasants, trussed as for chickens
4 slices streaky bacon
8 oz. chuck steak
1 dessertspoon seasoned flour
fried breadcrumbs
bread sauce, see page 149
red currant jelly

Wipe the birds with soft cloth; sprinkle inside and out with salt and pepper. Tie two slices of bacon over each bird. Divide the steak and put a piece inside the body of each bird; the meat is meant to keep the birds moist and juicy; it is not eaten but it makes excellent soup or can be added to stew or mince. Place birds in roasting tin, put a little butter or bacon fat in tin and roast in hot oven (450°F. or Gas Mark 7), for 45–50 minutes, basting from time to time. When nearly done, remove the bacon, baste well, dredge with seasoned flour and return to oven to get a good brown. To serve, remove trussing strings and place birds on a bed of watercress.

Fix two of the male pheasants' tail feathers in the end of the bird. Serve with a little red wine, fried breadcrumbs, bread sauce and red currant jelly.

ROAST GROUSE

Preparation time 15–20 minutes
Cooking time 30 minutes
To serve 2

You will need

1 brace young grouse, plucked and trussed, as for chicken
salt and pepper
2 oz. butter

Roast grouse

4 rashers streaky bacon
the cooked livers of birds
2 slices toast
1 dessertspoon seasoned flour

Wipe the birds with a soft cloth; sprinkle inside
and out with salt and pepper. Put 1 oz. butter
inside each; tie 2 thin rashers of bacon over the
breasts. Crush the cooked livers with a fork; season
with salt and pepper. Spread this on the toast;
put toast in roasting tin or casserole dish and put
the birds on top. Put in hot oven (425°F. or Gas
Mark 7) and roast 20–30 minutes, according to
size of birds; they should be slightly underdone,
but not 'rare'. Baste two or three times with bacon
fat and butter; 5 minutes before they are done,
remove the bacon, dredge lightly with flour and

put in a hot oven (425°F. or Gas Mark 7) to get
a good crust.
Serve on the slices of toast with bread sauce, see
page 149 and clear gravy made from the giblets.
It is not correct to serve vegetables with grouse
other than game chips and undressed watercress
and lettuce salad.

PARTRIDGES

For roasting, partridges should be shot in the same
year as bred and should not hang for more than
three or four days. They are roasted in the same
way as grouse, taking 30–35 minutes, and are
served with the same accompaniments.

GAME MEATS

Hare and venison are the best known of game meats
in Britain. Venison is the culinary name for all
breeds of deer, and the free ranging forest deer
from Scotland are considered the choicest. Efforts
have been made to rear deer on farms, but they

are not a success. Such venison is coarse and tasteless
compared with that from free deer from the forests
and hills. Venison should be hung at least 14 days;
longer if the weather is cold. If you are buying
venison be sure to ask if it has been hung and is
ready for cooking. Only the haunch, leg and loin
are suitable for roasting.

ROAST VENISON

Preparation time 2½ hours,
                    including marinating time
Cooking time   2½ hours
To serve   8–10

You will need

leg of venison, fillet end, 6–7 lb.
marinade, see below
venison pastry, see opposite

FOR THE MARINADE

¼ pint (U.S. ⅝ cup) vinegar
¼ pint (U.S. ⅝ cup) olive oil
1 small onion, sliced
1 teaspoon chopped fresh thyme
1 teaspoon chopped parsley
1 bay leaf, crushed
grating of nutmeg
1 teaspoon salt
¼ teaspoon black pepper

FOR THE VENISON PASTRY

2 lb. flour
pinch salt
4 oz. lard
cold water to mix to a stiff dough

After hanging the venison, trim it, rinse it and
dry thoroughly.
Mix all the ingredients for the marinade.
Lay venison on dish and pour marinade over. Let
it stand for 2 hours turning it and basting it with
marinade often.

TO MAKE PASTRY

Mix flour and salt, rub in lard, and mix it to
a pliable dough with cold water. Take venison
from marinade, wipe it.
Roll out pastry and wrap venison in it, sealing
edges well. Put in roasting tin and roast at (400°F.
or Gas Mark 6) for 2–2½ hours.
Remove the crust and serve venison with wine
sauce, see page 149, and red currant sauce, see
page 149.

JUGGED HARE

Preparation time 45 minutes
Cooking time 3–3½ hours
To serve 6–8

You will need

1 hare
2–3 carrots
1 large onion
2 small white turnips
6 cloves
2 heaped tablespoons flour
1 teaspoon salt
4 oz. butter
bunch herbs, sprig thyme, parsley, 2 bay leaves,
  2 sage leaves, 12 peppercorns, tied in muslin
strip lemon rind
4 oz. black mushrooms
1 wine glass port wine
1½–2 pints (U.S. 3¾–5 cups) stock *or* water
red currant jelly
forcemeat balls

The 'jug' used to be an old 7 lb. stone pickle or
jam jar; today you can use a modern earthenware
casserole, or a heavy copper one.
Traditionally it is served in the 'jug' in which it
is cooked.
The hare should be cut into small joints. The legs
of a hare can be quite large; they are cut into 3
or 4 pieces each. The body will make 6 or 8 pieces.
Peel carrots and turnips and slice them; peel onion
and stick with cloves. Mix flour and salt. Coat well
washed pieces of hare with this. Heat butter in
a thick saucepan and lightly fry hare in it. Put
them as they are fried in the casserole or stew jar,
scattering the vegetables among them, putting the
onion stuck with cloves in the middle of the pieces.
Lastly add the herbs, lemon rind and cleaned
mushrooms. Add the stock or water with a little
of the blood (2 or 3 tablespoons or more; it is all

a matter of taste) and the port wine. Cover closely
and cook in a moderate oven (350°F. or Gas
Mark 4) for 3–3½ hours.

FORCEMEAT BALLS FOR JUGGED HARE

Preparation time 20–25 minutes
Cooking time 10–15 minutes
To serve 6–8

You will need

8 oz. brown breadcrumbs
4 oz. shredded suet
1 medium-sized onion, finely chopped
1 dessertspoon chopped parsley
1 tablespoon fresh sage, thyme, marjoram mixed
  and finely chopped, or half quantities dried
  herbs
grated rind of ½ lemon
salt and pepper
little stock made from hare trimmings
½ glass port wine
2–3 oz. butter

Mix all dry ingredients and bind stiffly with stock
and port wine. Take up small quantities in the
floured hand, squeeze until mixture is bound
together; on a floured board roll each portion into
a ball, about the size of a walnut. Heat butter in
frying pan and fry the balls until lightly browned
all over, turning often.
When hare is done remove the herbs and the lemon
rind. Give it a good stir, and add forcemeat balls.
Return to oven for a few minutes to get thoroughly
hot. If the gravy has dried out in cooking, add
a little more boiling stock.
Serve with red currant sauce, see page 149.

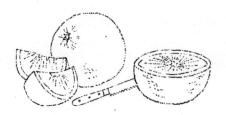

Roast duck with orange sauce

Grilled buttered halibut with tomato cream sauce

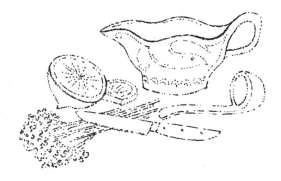

FISH

The British Isles is a group of islands surrounded by seas rich with fish.

The islands are relatively small so that no town is far inland and you can be pretty certain that all the fish you get anywhere is still fresh enough to 'taste of the sea'.

In fact I often tell visiting friends unused to our menus, 'When in doubt, choose fish'.

Apart from sea fish our lakes, ponds, rivers and some canals, abound with fish; and in many parts of the country it is still free for the catching.

Fishing with rod and line in still the working man's sport and any Saturday or Sunday you can see them sitting at the waterside, on little stools, patiently waiting for a bite.

Our fish is so good that the most simple methods of cooking suit it best; there is no need to disguise its natural flavour with highly seasoned sauces, or strongly flavoured herbs.

These should always be used judiciously to enhance the flavour of the fish rather than to give it a different flavour.

There are local associations attached to fish just as there are with cakes and pies. Greenwich has its annual whitebait feast; there are the oyster feasts of Colchester and Whitstable, while the Cockney loves his jellied eels and winkles.

The mussel, cockle and whelk stalls flourish at Southend. Any Cornish fishing village will produce its own version of star-gazy pie when the pilchards come in. Hastings still has its Winkle Club, of which the late Sir Winston Churchill was a member, though its members meet for social occasions rather than to just eat winkles!

FILLETS OF PLAICE WITH MUSHROOM SAUCE

Preparation time 20–25 minutes
Cooking time 35–40 minutes
To serve 4

You will need

1 large *or* 2 small plaice, about 2 lb., filleted and cut into 4 fillets
2 oz. butter
mushroom sauce, see page 148

Wipe fish and place in a shallow well buttered ovenware dish. Dot with the 2 oz. butter. Cover and bake in a moderate oven (350°F. or Gas Mark 4) for 20 minutes.

Remove to serving dish and keep warm.

Pour sauce over the fillets of plaice, garnish with sprigs of parsley and serve very hot.

Note

Plaice are in season all the year round, but are at their best towards the end of May.

GRILLED BUTTERED HALIBUT WITH TOMATO CREAM SAUCE

(Illustrated in colour on page 48)

Preparation time 30 minutes
Cooking time 30–35 minutes
To serve 6

You will need

6 halibut steaks, ¾–1-inch thick, about 2½ lb.
4 oz. butter
salt and pepper
4 tablespoons fine dry breadcrumbs

FOR THE SAUCE

2 oz. butter
1 small onion, chopped
4 medium-sized tomatoes, skinned
   and de-seeded
1 dessertspoon chopped parsley
1 teaspoon chopped chives
1 teaspoon chopped thyme
1 teaspoon chopped tarragon
good pinch salt
sprinkling of white pepper
1 level dessertspoon flour
2 tablespoons milk
½ pint (U.S. 1¼ cups) white wine and water
   or fish stock, half and half
1 teaspoon lemon juice
1 egg yolk
2 tablespoons thin cream

GARNISH

sprigs parsley
lemon slices
halved tomatoes

Wipe the fish, melt 3 oz. butter and brush both sides of the fish steaks with it. Place on grid in grill pan; fix grill pan under the red hot griller so that it is about 1-inch from the heat. Grill 6–7 minutes, or until fish is lightly browned. Sprinkle with salt and pepper, then turn to second sife. If necessary, brush over again with melted butter, place under griller and grill until lightly browned. As halibut is a very firm close textured fish it should not be placed too near the heat so that it browns before it is cooked through. Sprinkle second side with salt and pepper when done.
While fish is grilling mix the breadcrumbs with remaining butter, melted; any butter left over

from brushing fish can be added too. Spread these buttered crumbs over the second side of the fish when done, return it to the griller for 1–2 minutes, until the crumbs are browned and crisp.
Place fish on a hot serving dish; garnish with parsley, lemon slices and halved tomatoes. Serve tomato cream sauce in sauceboat.

TO MAKE SAUCE

Melt butter in saucepan, fry chopped onion 3 minutes, add 3 tomatoes, parsley and other herbs salt and pepper, and cook gently 3–4 minutes or until tomatoes are soft. Stir well to break up tomatoes. Add flour blended to a smooth cream with the 2 tablespoons milk, stir over low heat until boiling, add the white wine and water or stock and lemon juice. Add remaining tomato cut into small dice. Stir well, remove pan from heat and allow sauce to cool considerably. Beat egg yolk into cream and when the sauce has cooled, stir the cream and egg mixture slowly into it. The sauce must not be allowed to get near boiling after egg and cream are added, or it will curdle.

STUFFED COD CUTLETS

Preparation time 15 minutes
Cooking time 25 minutes
To serve 4

You will need

4 cod cutlets
juice of ½ lemon
1 onion
½ oz. butter
1 oz. breadcrumbs
¼ teaspoon tarragon
1 dessertspoon milk
4 pieces aluminium foil 9-inches square

Season cutlets with salt and pepper and sprinkle with a little of the lemon juice. Chop onion finely and cook in butter until transparent. Add the breadcrumbs, tarragon, milk, salt and pepper and remaining lemon juice. Form into 4 balls and put in centre of cutlets. Place the pieces of foil on a baking tin and arrange a cutlet in the centre of each. Fold over the sides of foil to overlap slightly in the middle and make a double fold in each end. Bake in the centre of a moderate oven (350°F, or Gas Mark 4) for 20 minutes.

Stuffed cod cutlets

HADDOCK WITH SHRIMP SAUCE

(Illustrated in colour on page 57)

Preparation time 15 minutes
Cooking time 30–35 minutes
To serve 4

You will need

1 fresh haddock, 2 lb., filleted
2–3 oz. butter
juice of ½ lemon
2 tablespoons milk
salt and pepper
2–3 lemon slices, to garnish
1 dessertspoon cornflour

FOR THE SAUCE

¼ pint (U.S. ⅝ cup) milk
½ pint (U.S. 1¼ cups) fish stock
1 dessertspoon anchovy essence
1 can shrimps *or* ½ pint (U.S. 1¼ cups) fresh shrimps
dash of pepper
few drops red colouring, if necessary
parsley
lemon butterflies

Simmer the bones and trimmings from the fish in ½ pint (U.S. 1¼ cups) salted water, with 1 onion added, to make fish stock.
Wash and dry fish. Place in well buttered fireproof dish, squeeze over the lemon juice, sprinkle with salt and pepper and dot with butter. Pour in the milk. Cover with greased paper or foil and bake in moderately hot oven (375°F. or Gas Mark 5) for 25–30 minutes. Strain off the liquor, and add it to the fish stock to make up to ½ pint (U.S. 1¼ cups). Keep fish hot while making sauce.

TO MAKE SAUCE

Blend cornflour to a paste with little milk. Put remaining milk and fish stock on to boil; when boiling pour over blended cornflour stirring all the time. Return to saucepan, stir over low heat until boiling point is reached, then add the anchovy essence and a dessertspoon of chopped shrimps. Add a dash of pepper (no salt) and stir over low heat 2–3 minutes. If a deeper pink is required, add few drops red colouring. Pour a little around fish and put remainder in sauceboat. Garnish with the remaining shrimps, lemon butterflies and a little chopped parsley.

IN-SHORE FISH

BAKED SPRATS

The sprats should be silvery bright, and their eyes clear and shining. If really fresh from the sea they can be cooked with the heads on, but when a day or two old, the heads should be removed drawing the entrails with them. Wash and dry the sprats, dust them with flour mixed with a little salt and pepper. Well grease a baking tin with dripping, put the sprats in, in neat rows, add a very little water and vinegar and dot pieces of dripping over

the fish. Bake in a hot oven (400°F. or Gas Mark 6) for 10–13 minutes. Dust with a little cayenne, and serve with pieces of lemon.

FRIED SPRATS

After cleaning and gutting the fish, dry them and toss in seasoned flour. Put them in a frying basket and fry in deep fat until well browned. Drain well on kitchen paper, and serve with cayenne and pieces of lemon, and thin brown bread and butter. Sprats can also be dipped in batter and fried in deep fat.

STUFFED HERRINGS

Preparation time 30 minutes
Cooking time 30 minutes
To serve 4

You will need

4 large, boned herrings
4 tablespoons white breadcrumbs
1 medium-sized onion, finely chopped
1 teaspoon chopped parsley
½ teaspoon mixed herbs
1 oz. margarine, melted
1 dessertspoon vinegar
½ teaspoon salt
¼ teaspoon pepper
extra margarine and crumbs for sprinkling

Wipe fish and sprinkle flesh sides with a little salt.
Mix breadcrumbs, onion, parsley and herbs, stir
in the melted margarine and bind stiffly with
vinegar. Spread this stuffing on the herrings, season,
and roll up from the head ends. Pack tightly in
a shallow fireproof dish, dot with margarine and
sprinkle with browned breadcrumbs. Bake in a
moderately hot oven (400°F. or Gas Mark 6), for
35–40 minutes. Serve hot. If liked, the herrings
can be kept whole and the stuffing placed in the
cavity left after removing the insides and roes.
Stitch up the opening, after stuffing, with strong
threads, leaving two loose ends of thread so it can
be pulled out after the fish is baked. Pipe a border
of duchesse potato, see page 63 around the edge

of the serving dish, sprinkle with cayenne pepper.
Arrange herrings on dish and garnish with lemon
butterflies and parsley sprigs.

BAKED STUFFED MACKEREL

Preparation time 20–25 minutes
Cooking time 25 minutes
To serve 4

You will need

1 mackerel, about 2 lb.
salt and pepper
½ pint (U.S. 1¼ cups) breadcrumbs
½ teaspoon mixed herbs
1 teaspoon chopped parsley
1 tablespoon peeled shrimps
beaten egg *or* milk
little margarine *or* dripping
lemon, tomatoes and cucumber, to garnish

Wash mackerel well, removing the head. Make
four deep gashes through the fish from the back.
Season with salt and pepper. Mix the breadcrumbs,
herbs and shrimps, reserve a few shrimps for
garnishing and moisten with beaten egg or milk.
Arrange the fish on baking dish and pack the
stuffing in the gashes, piling it well up. Dot with
margarine or dripping, cover with greaseproof
paper or aluminium foil and bake in moderate
oven (350°F. or Gas Mark 4), for 20–25 minutes.
Garnish with sliced lemon, tomato, cucumber and
a few whole shrimps.

FRIED HERRINGS, SCOTS STYLE

The herrings may be filleted or left whole. Season
them with salt and pepper and dip each in medium
oatmeal, pressing it on well with palette knife. Fry
them in butter or pork dripping, if filleted 2–3
minutes each side; if whole, allow 4–5 minutes
each side. Serve with quarters of lemon, and a knob
of butter on each herring.

Note

Herring roes can be fried separately in a little
butter, placed on buttered toast and served as a
supper dish.

JELLIED EELS, LONDON

The eel is not a deep sea fish, but it spends quite a lot of its life in salt water, in the estuaries of tidal rivers. Those from the Thames estuary are considered the best; jellied eels have always been a Cockney speciality.

Preparation time 30–40 minutes
Cooking time 1¼ hours
To serve 4

You will need

2 lb. eels, skinned and cleaned by the fishmonger
1 onion, chopped
1 carrot, chopped
1 small turnip, sliced
6 peppercorns
4 pints (U.S. 10 cups) fish stock made from fish trimmings and bones
1 cow heel *or* calf's foot
¼ pint (U.S. ⅝ cup) tarragon vinegar
squeeze lemon juice
½ oz. gelatine

Cut the eels into 2-inch chunks. Boil the vegetables and peppercorns in the fish stock for about 20 minutes; leave to go cold. Soak the eels in this stock overnight. Boil the well chopped cow heel or calf's foot in water to well cover and salt added, for 1½–2 hours to get a jellied stock. Put the pieces of eel in a pan, strain the marinade in which they were soaked, and the stock from the cow heel or calf's foot over them, add the vinegar and lemon juice and simmer 1 hour. Remove the eels to a deep dish, strain the liquor in which they cooked and add the gelatine dissolved in a little hot stock. Pour over the eels and leave to set.

FRESH WATER FISH

BAKED CARP

Preparation time 30 minutes
Cooking time 40 minutes
To serve 6–7

You will need

1 small onion, finely chopped
1 carrot, sliced
2 tomatoes, skinned and chopped
2 oz. butter, melted
1 medium-sized carp, about 4 lb.
1 tablespoon finely chopped parsley
1 tablespoon Worcestershire sauce
1 tablespoon lemon juice
salt, pepper

Mix the vegetables and place in a dish with the melted butter. Wash the fish, clean and scale it, removing the gall stone from the head. Place on top of the vegetables in dish and sprinkle with the parsley, Worcestershire sauce and the lemon juice. Season well with salt and pepper. Bake uncovered in a moderate oven (350°F. or Gas Mark 4), for 30–40 minutes basting frequently with the liquor in the dish. Serve from the dish with the vegetables and liquor.

SALMON SLICES IN ASPIC

Preparation time 15 minutes, aspic made in advance
Cooking time 30–40 minutes, including decoration
To serve 3–4

You will need

3 slices salmon, 6–8 oz. each
½ pint (U.S. 1¼ cups) liquid aspic, made with aspic jelly crystals
1 tomato
little cucumber
parsley, to garnish

Wash the salmon, dry well, sprinkle with salt and pepper and a few drops lemon juice. Wrap them in muslin and place in steamer over boiling water, cover closely and steam for 15–20 minutes according to thickness of slices. Take up, remove skin, and leave fish to cool. When cold, pour a thin layer of aspic over fish, put a small slice of tomato over centre bone and arrange slices of cucumber and parsley sprigs either side. Place on serving dish and leave until aspic is set and garnishing firmly fixed. Then coat with cool, but liquid aspic, allowing it to run over sides of fish to surround it. Leave to set.

SALMON TROUT

The salmon trout should rightly be called the sea trout; it is a sea fish but comes into fresh water to spawn.

It is never as red as the salmon, and seldom grows to more than 3 lb. in weight, but it is a true delicacy and valued by many gourmets as superior to salmon. All the ways of cooking salmon are suitable for it, but to boil it is to ruin it. To serve whole, hot or cold in aspic, it is very much better baked, in a moderate oven.

Preparation time 20 minutes, aspic ready
in advance
Cooking time 1½ hours
To serve 6

You will need

1 salmon trout, 3 lb.
¼ pint (U.S. ⅝ cup) red wine
2 tablespoons water
1 bay leaf
½–¾ pint (U.S. 1¼–1⅞ cups) liquid aspic, made
with aspic jelly crystals
softened butter for piping

GARNISH

lettuce
sliced tomato
sliced cucumber
sprigs parsley

Wash and clean fish, the fishmonger will do this for you, keeping the head on.

Put in a shallow ovenware dish with the wine, water, salt and pepper to taste, and the bay leaf. Cover and bake in moderate oven (350°F. or Gas Mark 4), for 1–1½ hours, until tender.

Put on serving dish; remove the skin. Brush over with liquid aspic. Decorate with a piping of softened butter, sliced cucumber and triangles of skinned tomato. Allow these to set, then coat whole fish again with aspic jelly.

Leave to go quite cold, then garnish the dish with washed dried lettuce, sliced tomatoes and cucumber and parsley.

The method of decoration can be varied according to taste. and to the season.

TROUT IN BUTTER WITH ALMONDS

Preparation time 20 minutes
Cooking time 10–15 minutes
To serve 4

You will need

4 small trout, about 6 oz. each
2 tablespoons flour
½ teaspoon salt
pinch pepper
2–3 oz. butter
1 teaspoon chopped parsley
juice of 1 lemon
4 oz. blanched almonds, sliced

Clean the fish, then wash and dry them. Mix together the flour, salt and pepper, dip each fish in this and shake to remove surplus.

Melt butter in thick frying pan, lay in the fish, sprinkle with chopped parsley and the strained lemon juice. Cook gently until one side of the fish is browned, about 5 minutes, then turn and cook the other side. Lay them on a hot dish and keep them warm.

Toss the almonds in the liquor in the pan and spread over the trout.

Serve with thin brown bread and butter.

Trout in butter with almonds

SHELLFISH

TO DRESS A CRAB

Break off the large claws and thin legs by twisting. Lay the crab on its back and pull out the flap or 'apron', bringing with it the body portion. Discard the stomach bag near the mouth and the grey, feathery gills, known as 'dead man's fingers'; these are not edible.

Split the body into small pieces with a pointed knife and from the honeycomb-like sections pick out as much meat as possible, putting it in a basin. Put the dark, paste like meat, the liver of the crab, in a separate basin. Crack claws and legs with a hammer or weight; remove meat from upper joints of the legs, using a skewer and mix it with the white meat from the body. Reserve the thin ends of legs with their tiny claws for garnishing. Remove flesh from the large claws and keep it whole to decorate finished crab.

Wash empty shell and dry it well. Chip off under portion of the shell to about ½-inch from the edge, there is a faint line round the shell which shows you how far to chip. Rub the outsides of the shell with a little olive oil or butter to give a smooth, attractive finish.

Chop the white meat in the basin and mix it with a few dry, white breadcrumbs, about a table-spoon, and season with salt, pepper, chopped parsley and prepared mustard, and a little vinegar. Be careful not to make it too wet. Season the dark meat with salt and pepper and a few breadcrumbs, sufficient to make a fairly firm paste.

Put the white meat into the shell and the prepared dark meat down the middle. Garnish with lines of chopped parsley, chopped yolk of hard-boiled egg and a sprinkling of paprika pepper. Cut the meat from the large claws into small triangles and arrange them along side the dark meat. Garnish dish with lemon quarters and the small claws.

LOBSTERS

All lobsters are a dull bluish or blackish green before they are boiled; the red colour comes with boiling.

Medium-sized lobsters are best for flavour and for tenderness, 2½–3 lb. is a good average weight. The flesh of the male lobster is firmer and better flavoured than that of the female. The hen, how-ever, contains the roe or 'coral' which is valued for sauces and garnishing.

The most simple way of serving lobster, and perhaps the nicest when the lobster is young and really well boiled, is dressed on the half shell. Twist off the large and small claws and crack them. Split the lobster down the centre from the underside with a strong, pointed knife. Remove the dark thread, spinal cord, from near the outer edge of the lobster, and discard the stomach which lies near the head, and the gills. If it is a hen lobster, take out the coral, roe, and use this as a garnish. Ease the meat in the tail away from the shell without removing it, and with a stainless or silver knife, cut it into ½-inch sections so that it can be easily lifted out. Mix the coral with a little salt and pepper and a squeeze of lemon juice and pile it near the head.

Put the halves of lobster on a bed of lettuce on a dish. Remove the meat from the large claws and arrange on lettuce. Garnish with the smaller claws, and supply lobster picks or metal skewers so that the eaters can pick the meat for themselves from the claws; these tit-bits are the tenderest and most delicious part of the lobster. Serve with mayonnaise, see page 148, and oil and vinegar.

PRAWNS AND SHRIMPS

There is no better way of eating these than just plain boiled, with brown bread and butter. Each eater should shell his or her own portion and it depends on the dexterity of each one as to who eats the biggest share.

POTTED SHRIMPS

The shrimps are kept whole and heated thoroughly in butter. Then put into small pots and covered with melted butter and left to go cold; they will keep several days in a cool place.

Note

Potted shrimps may be served as a first course or on plain biscuits. They are also good in brown bread sandwiches.

COCKLES, WHELKS AND WINKLES

These are specialities of the Essex coast towns and around the mouth of the Thames, though you will find 'whelk stalls' in many market towns and on fair grounds all over the country. Seldom do people sit down and make a proper meal of these shellfish; the eaters buy them in small saucers, doused with vinegar, and eat them with their fingers, standing round the stalls. Of course you can buy them in their shells around seaside towns, but not often in inland fishmongers.

Winkles are not so popular now as they used to be. The Cockney worker enjoyed his ½ pint (U.S. 1¼ cups) winkles on Saturdays and Sundays when he had the time to sit and 'winkle' them out with a pin, and many of the old London pubs used to sell them.

SMOKED AND SALTED FISH

It is not surprising that in a country abounding in fish the curing and preserving of it early became an important culinary art; it is an art in which we excel in the British Isles today, even though we have the means of keeping fish in its natural state for quite a considerable time. What was started as a means of preventing waste in times of glut and plenty is kept up because our smoked fish is delicious and justly world famous. In fact it is an important export.

Smoked salmon is the aristocrat and in the most demand, though smoked eels and smoked trout (not so expensive), are, in the opinion of many who really know good eating, more delicious and superior. Myself, I go for smoked trout first. Smoked cods' roe is preferred by many to its superior foreign relation, caviare. All these smoked delicacies need no further cooking; they are served simply with thin brown bread and butter or toast, with a squeeze of lemon juice and dash of cayenne, if you wish. Bloaters are large, freshly caught herrings salted, smoked and half dried. They are salted first when smoked in wood smoke; the fishmonger then strings them up through their mouths and hangs them in his shop to dry. Yarmouth bloaters are considered the best, simply because the herrings arrive at the east coast when they are their fattest and best, in the late autumn. Bloaters are best grilled in front of an open fire; I remember in Yorkshire we used to put them between a double grid iron which was suspended on the bars in front of the kitchen fire; the iron was turned when the first side was done. They can be grilled under the modern gas or electric grill, spread with a little butter, or they are quite good fried in butter or bacon fat.

Kippers are split, salted and smoked herrings; they can be grilled or pan fried, and nothing should be added to them but a little butter and they need no longer than 5 minutes each side.

The Findon or Finnan haddock came originally from Findon in Scotland, and is perhaps the favourite of all smoked fish. More commonly known as 'Finny Haddie' it is unbeatable for its soft, tender flesh and delicate flavour. It is a near rival of bacon and eggs as *the* British breakfast dish. It is best when smoked and cooked on the bone; smoked haddock fillets are having a fight to win favour but they are a poor, thin relation of the noble finny. And don't be put off by the boneless yellow dyed substitutes, mainly cat fish, that are quite expensive, but a different thing entirely from the real creamy fleshed smoked haddock.

The cooking of Finny Haddie is quick and simple. Just wash it, lay it in a buttered frying pan, cover it with milk and water, half and half, put a lid on top of the pan and let it simmer 8–10 minutes according to thickness. To serve, place on a hot plate with a little of the 'gravy' poured over and a knob of butter on top.

'Egganhaddie' is a great favourite in the North; a poached egg is placed on top.

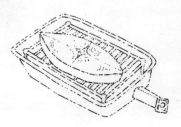

Haddock with shrimp sauce

Garden produce

VEGETABLES

Vegetables have never been so important to the British as their meat or fish, except, of course, to vegetarians. To the housewife, and I am afraid to many hoteliers, the meat is the thing and the vegetable course is a hit-or-miss affair. This is a pity since we grow good, deliciously flavoured vegetables in gardens and allotments, and commercially; but between the garden and the table awful things can happen to them. The trouble is, water, and a lack of imagination. Everything must be boiled in a bath of water, usually too long. Our garden peas, beans, spinach, asparagus, cauliflowers and broccoli, potatoes, particularly when new, are good enough to be served as courses in themselves. Why are beets usually boiled and served cold in vinegar? They are delicious buttered as a hot vegetable.

Oddly enough many of the 'speciality' vegetables that are now freely obtainable, are more traditional than the usual varieties, though they were not always grown principally for the table, indeed some of them grew wild; others were handsome border plants. Salsify, for instance, known as oyster plant because of its salty, fishy flavour, has tall purplish pink flowers and makes a fine herbaceous border plant. The young leaves are good in salad; it is the roots that are eaten as a vegetable. Sea kale used to grow wild in sandy, pebbly soil near the sea, where its slender stalks were self branching; it is one of our oldest vegetables. Globe artichokes are a splendid border plant and whether the artichokes grew to a gathering size or not, did not, in the old days, seem to matter. The Jerusalem artichoke with its knobbly roots like mis-shapen potatoes was in many country gardens used as a hedge or screen growing to four to five feet in height. Asparagus too, was allowed to grow in its own sweet way or in a wild state. Besides, to grow any quantity of asparagus meant keeping a large bed for many years; it could not be alternated with other vegetables so was uneconomical in small gardens. That is one reason, too, why it is so expensive now it is grown commercially. All vegetables to taste their best should be gathered young and eaten fresh.

GENERAL HINTS ON COOKING AND SERVING

BROAD BEANS

Choose small, young beans; rinse in cold water after shelling. Add a few of the youngest, tenderest pods, broken into small pieces. Put in boiling water to just cover. Add salt when beans are nearly done. When tender, 10–15 minutes, according to age and size, drain well.

Return all to saucepan add a walnut sized piece of butter for each 2 lb. beans and a teaspoon chopped parsley. Shake pan over low heat until all beans are coated with butter and parsley.

The broad bean pods improve the flavour. If beans are old, the skins will have to be removed and discarded after cooking.

GARDEN PEAS

After shelling, rinse in running cold water. Put into boiling salted water to just cover them, with a sprig of mint. Boil gently 15–20 minutes. Drain well, remove mint. Put peas back in pan with a knob of butter and sprinkling of chopped mint. Toss over low heat until peas are well coated with butter.

KIDNEY OR DWARF BEANS

Cut off stalk and flower ends; small beans can be cooked whole. Snap larger ones into 2 or 3 pieces. Boil gently in salted water to cover, 15–20 minutes. Drain in colander when tender, return to pan with knob of butter, toss until beans are well coated.

RUNNER BEANS

These are bigger and coarser in texture than dwarf beans, so they are usually cut into strips lengthwise or diagonally after topping and tailing and removing any strings. After preparation, cook as for dwarf beans.

PURPLE SPROUTING BROCCOLI

This lovely looking vegetable grows in small sprouts from the main stem, though the top of the plant grows as big as a small cauliflower. When cooked it turns a deep, rich green. After trimming off the thickest stalk ends, the sprigs and leaves are cooked whole in boiling salted water until tender, and after straining are served with small pieces of butter on top. The smaller sprigs should have an asparagus like taste.

Buttered baked potatoes

BUTTERED BAKED POTATOES

Scrub the potatoes well, removing all blemishes from skins, and make a slit across top of each, to prevent bursting. Rub skins with butter or oil. Bake in a moderate oven (350°F. or Gas Mark 4) until soft when pinched. Make a cross in the skin, squeeze the potato gently to widen the cross and push some of the interior out; put a knob of butter and sprinkling of salt and pepper on top; sprinkle with chopped chives.

BUTTERED CAULIFLOWER AND HEADING BROCCOLI

Boil the cauliflower or broccoli whole. To prevent breakage, wrap it in muslin. Take up carefully, drain well, and place flower side uppermost in serving dish. Melt 1 oz. butter, pour over the cauliflower and serve very hot.

BUTTERED SPINACH

After washing spinach in several waters and removing stalks and coarse veins, put it in a pan with only the water clinging to it. Cover closely and simmer 10–12 minutes. Strain in a colander, pressing it well with a saucer to remove as much water as possible. Then return to the pan, add a good knob of butter, season well with salt and pepper, and toss spinach over low heat until every leaf is coated with butter. Serve very hot. Allow 2 lb. to 2 people.

BUTTERED BEETS

Baby beets, no bigger than a golf ball, are best. Skins of the beets should be unbroken; twist off the tops, do not cut them. Boil until tender, 10–15 minutes according to size. Drain and when cool enough to handle, remove the skins. For a dozen or so beets, melt 2 oz. butter in saucepan and toss the beets in this over low heat until all the beets are coated. Season well with salt and pepper. Large beets may be cut into slices or diced, and buttered; they will, of course, take longer to cook than the baby beets.

YOUNG MARROWS

They need not be peeled or seeded and can be cooked whole; if larger than 8–9-inches, they should be quartered, peeled and seeds removed. They are best baked in a casserole in a moderate oven (350°F. or Gas Mark 4), with a little milk, salt, pepper and butter added. The liquor from the marrow can then be used to make a good white sauce which should be poured over the marrow in the casserole when serving. If you have to boil the marrow, do it in as little water as possible, and be careful not to overcook, 15–20 minutes is usually long enough. When done, take up the marrow with a draining spoon, letting all water drip away. Place one or two slices of toast in the bottom of a vegetable dish and arrange the marrow on top; the toast absorbs surplus moisture and is not meant to be eaten. Coat marrow with white sauce, see page 148 or serve sauce separately.

BRUSSELS SPROUTS

These are the most delicate of the cabbage family, and they grow to perfection in this country. To preserve their lovely green colour they should be dropped into fast boiling salted water, boiled quickly 10–15 minutes, drained well, seasoned with pepper, and tossed in butter.

SPRING CABBAGE

The first of the season's green vegetables are so tender that they need only short cooking to preserve the rich dark green. There is usually very little waste with spring greens, and the darkest outside leaves should be used, the thick middle rib removed. The leaves should be roughly torn up, and the heart cut into halves or quarters, after well washing, and boiled quickly in as little water as possible until tender. Then drain well, chop and season them and serve at once. All greens should be served immediately they are cooked; they soon develop a stale taste.

Cabbages and Savoys have less flavour than spring greens and it is easy to reduce them to a flavourless mass. Here, conservative cooking is necessary to keep them crisp. They should be quartered, inner coarse stalks removed and the quarters shredded. Soak in salted water for a time to bring out insects etc. Drain and shake the cabbage well. Have ready a large pan, the bottom covered with about 1-inch boiling salted water, add the cabbage packing it well down, put on lid and boil rapidly 15 minutes. Drain in a colander, pressing cabbage with a plate and serve at once.

ENGLISH ASPARAGUS

Is at its best in June to July. It should be served as a separate dish, as a first course, or it can be served on a side plate to be eaten with the main course or immediately after. Cut off earthy ends of stalks and tie stalks in bundles of about a dozen. Wrap them in muslin. Place upright on stalk ends in a pan of boiling salted water, or lay them completely flat. Boil 15–20 minutes according to thickness. Take up, and allow to drain in the muslin, then place on a long, shallow dish. In serving, be careful not to break off the delicate tips.

Asparagus is always served simply, with oiled butter or Hollandaise sauce, see page 149.

GLOBE ARTICHOKES

These are another vegetable to be eaten as a separate course. This vegetable is rather like a round green water lily. The tips of the 'petals' should be trimmed with scissors if faded, and the stalk cut off. Then they are boiled in salted water until tender when a fork is pushed into the stalk end. Take up and drain on a napkin. Serve with butter or Hollandaise sauce, see page 149.

JERUSALEM ARTICHOKES

To 2 lb. artichokes allow 2 pints (U.S. 5 cups) water with a teaspoon of salt and a dessertspoon vinegar added. Wash and peel the artichokes, putting them at once into water and vinegar. Put them into the boiling water with vinegar and salt added, boil for 15 minutes then test with a fork. Allow a little longer if necessary, but do not overcook as they easily break and become discoloured. They can be mashed with salt, pepper and butter added, after draining well, or served in a hot dish and coated with a good white sauce, see page 148.

SALSIFY

This vegetable also has to be prepared quickly and placed in vinegar and water or lemon juice, and water, to preserve its colour. The long, tapering roots, rather like parsnips, should be scraped gently, cut into 3 or 4 pieces and dropped at once into water with vinegar or lemon juice. Put them into boiling water with salt and lemon juice added, boil them rapidly until tender and serve at once with creamy white sauce, see page 148.

SEA KALE

Cook in exactly the same way as asparagus, after removing the earthy ends, and serve with plain butter. It should be eaten as a separate vegetable.

ONIONS, BOILED

Have onions of equal size; if large, halve them. Blanch them and place in a saucepan with half milk and half water to well cover them, adding salt and pepper. Simmer until tender. Take up and serve in a soup plate with a little of the cooking liquor, pepper and salt, and a good piece of butter on top.

ONIONS, BRAISED

Peel medium-sized onions, blanch them, put into cold water with a teaspoon salt added, boil for ½ hour, then strain. Place in a baking dish with a little hot dripping in it, baste them well, cover and bake in a moderate oven (350°F. or Gas Mark 4) for 1–1½ hours, according to size, basting often. Coat with a good brown sauce, see page 148, and serve very hot.

LEEKS

These have the flavour of onions, but more delicate, are a most delicious vegetable. Usually only the white parts are used, but if the leeks are fresh, the green parts are quite good.
After trimming off roots and outer skin and faded tops, wash in several waters. If very thick, split them lengthwise, though it is best to avoid this as it causes the leeks to break during cooking. Place in boiling salted water and simmer until tender. Drain well and use the water with half quantity of milk to make white sauce, see page 148, to pour over the leeks.

MUSHROOMS

If to be fried, should not be washed; it is not necessary to peel them when they are fresh. Sprinkle the underside, the 'gills' with a little salt, leave for a while, then wipe off the melted salt with a cloth. Fry in hot bacon fat, after the bacon.

GRILLED MUSHROOMS

The flat mushrooms are the best. Prepare as for fried mushrooms. Grill the smooth side first, brushing over with a little melted fat. Then lay strips of bacon fat over the gills and grill for 3–4 minutes. The bacon can be grilled at the same time. When grilling the mushrooms with steak or cutlets, use pieces of fat from the meat to lay on the mushrooms. Sprinkle with salt and pepper to serve. Or they can be put in grill pan under meat, see page 24.

ROOT VEGETABLES

Old carrots, parsnips, turnips and swedes, are usually boiled or cooked in stews. All are improved if mashed with salt, pepper and butter added. The woody skins of turnips and swedes should be peeled thickly, parsnips should be peeled thinly and carrots should always be scraped. Parsnips are good baked round the meat, like potatoes, and go particularly well with roast beef.

BAKED STUFFED MARROW

Preparation time 20 minutes
Cooking time 45 minutes–1 hour
To serve 4

You will need

1 small marrow
4 oz. mushrooms, sliced
1 oz. butter
12 oz. cooked beef *or* tongue, chopped
1 teaspoon made mustard
salt and pepper
1 oz. Cheddar cheese, grated

CHEESEY MUSTARD SAUCE

1 oz. flour
¼ level teaspoon salt
1 level teaspoon dry mustard
1 oz. butter
½ pint (U.S. 1¼ cups) milk
3 oz. Cheddar cheese, grated
1 teaspoon vinegar
1 level teaspoon sugar

Slice off the top of the marrow, to make a lid and scoop out the seeds. Lightly fry mushrooms in butter, mix in meat and mustard and season well. Fill marrow with this mixture, sprinkle over cheese. Brush with melted butter and bake in a moderate oven (350°F. or Gas Mark 4) for 45 minutes to 1 hour, until marrow is soft.

Baked stuffed marrow

Sift together flour, salt and mustard. In a saucepan beat together the flour mixture with the butter for 2 minutes. Remove from heat and gradually blend in milk. Return to heat and bring to the boil, stirring as the sauce thickens. Add remaining ingredients, bring to the boil and serve with the marrow, garnished with cooked mixed vegetables.

DUCHESSE POTATOES

Preparation time	15–20 minutes, after boiling potatoes
Cooking time	10 minutes
To serve	4

You will need

2 lb. cooked potatoes
3 tablespoons milk
2 oz. butter
2 egg yolks, beaten
½ teaspoon salt
¼ teaspoon black pepper

Mash potatoes while hot. Heat milk and melt butter in it. Beat into potatoes, add egg yolks, salt and pepper. Beat until quite smooth. Put into forcing bag with large star tube; pipe rosettes or heaps to the size required on to a greased baking tray. Bake in hot oven (400°F. or Gas Mark 6), until lightly browned. Cool slightly on oven sheet before removing.

POTATO CHIPS (DEEP FRIED)

Preparation time	15–20 minutes
Cooking time	10–20 minutes, depending on how many are fried at a time
To serve	4

You will need

1½–2 lb. potatoes
1 pint (U.S. 2½ cups) melted lard, dripping *or* cooking oil
little salt

Wash and peel potatoes, cut into chips not more than ½-inch thick. Leave in water to cover for at least 1 hour; drain off water and dry thoroughly. Heat oil or fat in a thick saucepan (pan must not be more than half full, as fat boils up), to 360°F. or just before it gives off blue smoke. Test by dropping a chip in; it should rise to the top immediately if temperature is right. Put chips in frying basket in thin layer, lower heat under pan and put basket in; increase heat and cook chips 5–6 minutes. They will now be a pale gold colour. Take out of fat and empty them on to absorbent paper. Repeat until all the chips are cooked to this stage. Reheat fat and fry the chips a second time for about 2 minutes when they will be crisp and well browned.

COLCANNON OR BUBBLE AND SQUEAK

Preparation time	15 minutes
Cooking time	45 minutes
To serve	4

You will need

1 lb. mashed potatoes
1 lb. cooked greens, cabbage, savoy, kale, chopped
2 oz. melted butter *or* dripping
1 medium-sized onion, chopped
2–3 tablespoons browned breadcrumbs

Mix potatoes and chopped greens; season with salt and pepper if necessary. Heat butter or dripping in frying pan; fry onion in it until transparent, then add vegetables, stir and mix with onion and fat until thoroughly hot. Well grease a 2-pint pudding basin and line it with browned crumbs. Pack the vegetables into this, pressing firmly down. Cover with foil or greased paper and bake in hot oven (400°F. or Gas Mark 6), for 40–45 minutes. Turn out on a dish to serve.

Note

In the Yorkshire version of bubble and squeak the mixed vegetables are cooked in frying pan until brown on underside, then it is served from the pan, cut in wedges. This is regarded as a good way of heating up cold vegetables and it is usual to cook enough so that there will be some left-overs for bubble and squeak. When cooked in the frying pan cooking time is 15–20 minutes.

BRAISED CELERY

Preparation time 20 minutes
Cooking time 35 minutes
To serve 4

You will need

2 large heads celery
salt and pepper
½ pint (U.S. 1¼ cups) stock
4 rashers streaky bacon
¼ pint (U.S. ⅝ cup) thick brown sauce,
  see page 148

Trim celery, cut into quarters and wash well. Put in a well greased shallow fireproof dish, sprinkle with salt and pepper, and pour in half the stock. Remove rinds from bacon, and fry it lightly. Put pieces of bacon on top of celery, cover closely, and bake in hot oven (400°F. or Gas Mark 6) 30–35 minutes, or until tender when tested with fork. Take up, drain well, and place on hot dish. Add remain-ing stock to celery liquor, boil well to reduce, and stir in the brown sauce. Colour with a little gravy browning if necessary, and pour round the celery just before serving. Garnish with chopped parsley.

SALADINGS, HERBS AND SPICES

The usual salad greens used in this country are lettuce, watercress, mustard and cress and cucumber, spring onions, chives and radishes. Old saladings that are almost forgotten are young dandelion leaves, sorrel and radish pods. All salads are improved if a few herbs are put into the bottom of the bowl.

Spring onions in the salad are more typically British than garlic. Marigold petals, nasturtium leaves and seeds are used in many villages and country towns.

The salad served complete as it is today is a fairly new dish in Britain. It was much more usual to serve the green separately. And what is more British than cress and cucumber sandwiches for tea. It is an old British habit kept up today, to finish off lunch or dinner with a good tangy cheese, watercress, celery and radishes.

The skin of cucumber should not be removed when using it for sandwiches or in salads.

PARSLEY

Has endless uses in the kitchen, in sauces, soups and salads; mixed with butter for parsley butter to serve with fish; as a garnish for meat and fish; in stews and casseroles; add plenty of it, chopped, to old potatoes.

BAY LEAVES

These used fresh or dried are one of the most common herbs. They are used in stews or soups one small leaf used in a custard or milk pudding gives an aromatic flavour.

BASIL

This is a very strongly flavoured herb, aromatic, almost like cloves. It should be used sparingly in salads, soups, stews and tomato dishes. In its dried, powdered form, it is used in flavouring sausages.

CELERY SEED

This is used to give celery flavour to anything where fresh celery would be used in season.

CHERVIL

If finely chopped is excellent in soups, egg and fish dishes and salads.

DILL

This is a very pungent herb. Dill leaves are chopped and added to butter to make dill butter to serve with grilled lamb chops or cutlets. Dill flavoured white sauce is extra good with fish.

FENNEL

This is often mistaken for dill. The leaves are used with fish, in white sauce, or chopped and sprinkled on the cooked fish. The seeds are sometimes used in cakes or bread and in pickles.

MARJORAM

This has a yellowish green mint shaped leaf. It has a very strong flavour and should be used with care. Fresh, it gives a new flavour to salads. Dried, it can be used to flavour stuffings, stews, rissoles, minced meat, scrambled eggs.

MINT

Together with parsley, the herb in most common use in Britain. There are several kinds; the one in most gardens is spearmint.
Use with new potatoes and peas during boiling, and in mint sauce; a little added to a salad is good. It is an excellent addition to a fruit cup. Mint dries very well for winter use, or it can be made into mint sauce and bottled.

NASTURTIUM

The leaves are excellent chopped in a salad. The pickled seeds can be substituted for pickled capers.

ROSEMARY

Although still grown in many country gardens, is not used as much as it deserves to be. It is excellent, chopped and sprinkled over roast lamb or mutton before roasting, or over grilled steak and chops. When roasting a chicken put a spray of rosemary inside the bird.

SAGE

This is a strongly flavoured herb used in stuffings and savoury puddings.

SAVORY

(Winter and Summer) is used to flavour almost any savoury dish; it has been used in this country since Roman days and is an old fashioned flavouring for pork pies. It is often used when boiling broad beans, as mint is used with peas.

TARRAGON

With fine, feathery leaves, is used to flavour sauces, salads, stews and pickles.

THYME

This is generally known as a stuffing herb, and is, along with sage, the chief ingredient in mixed herbs sold in packets. It has a very strong flavour and scent, lemon thyme having a distinct lemon scent.

MIXED HERBS

The correct blend is two parts dried parsley, one of lemon thyme, one part marjoram, one part sage, one part winter savory, all blended after drying. Use sparingly.

FINES HERBES

Used for the popular omelette aux fines herbes, consists of equal quantities of fresh parsley, chives, tarragon or chervil, marjoram, a suggestion of thyme, all finely chopped.

BOUQUET GARNI

The traditional 'bunch of herbs'. Used for flavouring soups, stews, stock. Consists of a sprig of parsley, a bay leaf, sprig of thyme and marjoram, a few peppercorns, blade of mace, tied together in a piece of muslin. The bouquet is thrown away after the cooking.

ALLSPICE

The sun dried berry from West Indies, so called because it has a flavour that suggests several spices. Not to be confused with mixed cake spice, of which it forms a part. Used whole in pickles; in water in which meat and fish is boiled; ground in cakes, puddings, sweet sauces.

MIXED CAKE SPICE

This consists of ground cinnamon, cloves, nutmeg, allspice, ginger, caraway, pimento, coriander seeds. Used in rich fruit cakes, Christmas puddings, mincemeat.

MIXED PICKLING SPICE

An assortment of spices. Though chiefly used for making pickles, a few of them added to the water in which fish is boiled imparts a good flavour.

CARAWAY SEEDS

Usually associated with seed cake, but can be added to bread, and sprinkled on the top of loaves.

CLOVES

Most common use is in apple pie or baked apples, apple sauce. Spike the fat of ham or pork with cloves, when baking it. Use in spiced vinegar for pickled fruit; ground for flavouring cakes, chutneys.

PEPPERCORNS

(White and black) much better than ground, both in cooking and at the table, used in a pepper mill. Fresh ground peppercorns should be used in hotpots and bean casseroles. Whole peppercorns should always be used when making soups or stocks that must be kept clear; ground pepper clouds them.

CINNAMON

Aromatic bark of tree from Ceylon. Used in stick form for infusing in milk and other liquids for puddings, custards. Ground in cakes and puddings.

MACE

This is the husk that covers the nutmeg so it has a flavour rather like nutmeg, but milder. Infuse in soups, stews, fish boiling water, milk for sauces. Ground in cakes, gingerbreads and puddings.

NUTMEG

A hard, aromatic seed. Can be bought ground but the essential flavour is lost. Should be ground fresh over custards, junkets, milk puddings, into cakes. Try a pinch sprinkled over cauliflower, mashed potatoes, spinach and cabbage, and added to stews.

GINGER

Underground root, used whole in spiced vinegar for pickles; ground in small quantites in stews. Used in gingerbreads and puddings. Some people like it on melon.

VANILLA PODS

So much better than commercial vanilla essence bought in bottles. An inch or so of the pod is broken off and boiled with milk to infuse it for puddings, custards or for cake making.

SAFFRON

This is the dried stigma from the crocus; sold in blade form and powder. Gives pale yellow colour to cakes, biscuits and sauces.

TURMERIC

A spice root similar to ginger, but much milder and more aromatic. It is usually sold ground, and is used in pickles and sauces.

MUSTARD

Perhaps the most common spice used in Britain. But apart from being the accompaniment to roast beef, it is a good flavouring in soups and stews, and mustard sauce is served with both meat and fish dishes.

COUNTRY VEGETABLE SALAD

Preparation time 35–40 minutes
Cooking time no cooking
To serve 4

You will need

1 firm lettuce
1 bunch watercress
small celery heart
small bunch mustard and cress
6–8 spring onions
few chives
1 hard-boiled egg
2 sliced cooked carrots
2 oz. raw mushrooms, sliced
1 teaspoon chopped mint
1 teaspoon chopped parsley
½ cucumber, sliced
2 tablespoons cooked peas
mayonnaise, see page 148
oil and vinegar

Wash lettuce, separate outer leaves, cut heart into quarters; wash watercress, removing faded leaves; wash celery heart and cut into quarters. Wash mustard and cress in colander. Wrap these in a cloth to dry. Remove roots and outer skins of spring onion; wash chives if necessary; cut egg into quarters; slice carrots, wipe mushrooms, they need not be peeled if fresh, and cut into slices downwards. Sprinkle chopped mint and parsley over bottom of salad bowl; arrange lettuce and watercress around the bowl, and arrange other ingredients in groups on top. Serve with mayonnaise, and oil and vinegar.

VARIATION

CHEESE AND VEGETABLE SALAD

Use 4 oz. grated cheese in place of egg.

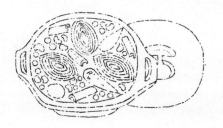

A selection of vegetables

HIGH TEA AND SUPPER DISHES

I believe that high tea is purely a British institution, at least I have never come across anything quite like it in any other country. It seems, too, that it is more of an institution in the North of England and Scotland than it is in the southern parts. When I first took a friend from London to tea in Yorkshire, around 5 o'clock he was a bit puzzled. 'But this is not tea' he said, 'It's a meal'. Then noticing the tea cups among the pies, potted meats, pressed tongue and salad and piles of bread and cakes, trifle and tarts, he went on 'You don't mean to say you drink *tea* with that lot. Barbarous! I'll never get through it!' But he did, and when four or five hours later a supper just as substantial came up, he managed that too. But doesn't it make a lot of work, many people ask. Well it did in the days when the housewife did everything herself. But it wasn't last minute work; the cold meats were made in advance. At one time the making of cold, pressed meats, potted meats and moulds, was a special accomplishment of the British housewife.

Now that we can buy practically everything in a can or packet it is still a good idea to make at least some of these cold meats, for they *do* taste better. And with modern equipment and refrigerators to keep food fresh for days, it's all so much easier for the housewife.

Though the foods for high tea and supper are mostly inter-changeable, it was more the custom to have cold for high tea and something hot for supper. The hot supper dishes were usually something quickly cooked or something that would 'look after itself' in the oven; or a pie would be made earlier in the day and heated up for supper. Sausages were great favourites, sausage and mash was always more a supper dish than a dinner dish in the North, and of course, the unbeatable fish and chips.

EGG AND BACON FLAN

Preparation time 35–40 minutes, including pastry
Cooking time 45 minutes
To serve 4

You will need

8 oz. flan pastry, see page 78
1 small onion, chopped
½ oz. butter
4 oz. bacon
2 eggs
¼ pint (U.S. 1¼ cups) milk
salt and pepper to taste

Roll out the pastry thinly and line an 8-inch flan ring or tart tin with it. Bake blind, see page 78 for 20 minutes in hot oven (400°F. or Gas Mark 6).

TO MAKE THE FILLING

Fry the onion in butter until golden brown. Cut rinds from bacon; cut bacon into strips and fry lightly. Beat eggs, pour in the milk and salt and pepper and stir well. Put onion and bacon all over bottom of the flan case; pour in egg and milk mixture. Bake in moderate oven (350°F. or Gas Mark 4), for 20–25 minutes or until custard is set. Garnish with a sprig of parsley.

LIVER AND BACON HOT-POT WITH FORCEMEAT BALLS

(Illustrated in colour on page 75)

Preparation time 30 minutes
Cooking time 2 hours
To serve 4–6

You will need

1 lb. pig's liver
12 oz. streaky bacon in the piece
1 large onion
1 tablespoon flour
¼ teaspoon salt
¼ teaspoon pepper
1 dessertspoon chopped parsley
1 teaspoon chopped sage
1 teaspoon chopped thyme

FOR THE FORCEMEAT

4 tablespoons breadcrumbs
2 tablespoons shredded suet
½ teaspoon salt
¼ teaspoon pepper
1 small onion, finely chopped
1 dessertspoon chopped mixed herbs, parsley, sage, thyme
milk *or* stock to bind

Cut liver into chunky pieces, removing skin and any pipes or gristle. Soak liver in salted water for about half an hour. Remove rind from bacon and cut six thin rashers from the piece. Cut rest into pieces about 1-inch square. Fry these in a deep frying pan or saucepan until lightly browned and a little fat is extracted. Peel and slice onion and fry it with the bacon until transparent. Remove bacon and onion to a casserole.

Mix flour with salt and pepper. Drain liver from salt water and dry in a cloth. Toss liver in flour until lightly coated, then fry in the bacon fat, stirring well, for 2–3 minutes. Remove liver into the casserole with the bacon and onion and stir well until liver and bacon are mixed, sprinkling in the herbs. Add a little water to the fat and juices extracted from the liver in frying pan and stir over low heat until boiling. Pour this over liver and bacon in casserole. Cover. Bake in a moderately hot oven (400°F. or Gas Mark 6), for 1½ hours, then remove the lid of casserole and arrange rashers on top of liver. Return to oven until rashers are crisp.

Country sausage and mash

TO MAKE THE FORCEMEAT BALLS

Mix the breadcrumbs, suet, salt, pepper, onion and herbs and mix to a crumbly mixture with a little milk or stock. Make it into small balls on a floured board. The forcemeat balls can be baked in the oven in a little fat or fried in the fat in the roasting tin until lightly browned. Arrange them around the meat in dish.

COUNTRY SAUSAGE AND MASH

Preparation time 20 minutes
Cooking time 20–25 minutes
To serve 4

You will need

1 lb. pork sausages
2 oz. cheese, grated
½ level teaspoon nutmeg
1½ lb. creamed potatoes
fried onion rings to garnish

Fry the sausages very slowly until cooked and evenly browned, approximately 20 minutes. Beat the grated cheese and nutmeg into the hot creamed potatoes and season if necessary. Place a layer of potato in a serving dish and place the sausages on top. With the remaining potato pipe a design around the sausages. Garnish with fried onion rings and serve.

MEAT AND TOMATO MOULD

Preparation time 30 minutes
Cooking time   45 minutes, including
                    filling mould
To serve   4–5

You will need

½ pint (U.S. 1¼ cups) packet aspic
1 oz. luxury margarine
8 oz. minced beef
1 large onion, finely chopped
salt and pepper
pinch mixed herbs
8 oz. tomatoes
4 oz. peas, cooked
4 oz. ham, thinly sliced
lettuce and parsley, to garnish

Prepare aspic according to instructions on the
packet and leave to cool. Melt margarine in frying
pan, fry mince and onion 10–15 minutes. Season
with salt, pepper and mixed herbs, leave to get
cold. Coat a 1 lb. loaf tin with aspic. Skin tomatoes,
cut into thin slices, dip these in aspic and line
the bottom and sides of the tin. Place half the mince
over tomatoes; add half the peas. Cut ham into
strips and cover peas. Add remaining peas and
then rest of mince. Press each layer down well
and cover with a coating of aspic. Leave to set in
a cool place. When set, turn out and garnish.

CORNISH PASTIES

(Illustrated in colour on page 75)

Preparation time 30 minutes
Cooking time   40 minutes
To serve   4

You will need

10 oz. short pastry, see page 77
12 oz. steak
4 oz. kidney
2 medium-sized raw potatoes
1 medium-sized onion
½ teaspoon salt
¼ teaspoon pepper
little stock *or* water
1 egg, beaten

Roll out pastry thinly and cut into rounds, using
a 5-inch saucepan lid as a guide, or cutting round
a 5-inch plate.
Cut steak and kidney into very small cubes. Peel
and dice potatoes; chop onion finely. Mix and
season with salt and pepper. Place about 2 tablespoons of mixture down centre of each circle
of pastry and sprinkle a little stock or water, about
3 tablespoons, over the mixture. Brush edges of
pastry with milk and draw the opposite sides of
circle together over top of the meat, pinching edges
very securely together and then fluting them by
pinching between finger and thumb. Brush over
with beaten egg and prick with a fork. Place on
a baking sheet and bake in hot oven (425°F. or
Gas Mark 7), for 10 minutes, then lower heat to
(350°F. or Gas Mark 4) and move pasties to
a lower shelf. Bake 30 minutes longer. Cover pasties
with paper if they get too brown.

PRESSED OX TONGUE

Preparation time 15–20 minutes, after soaking
Cooking time   2½ hours, plus 20 minutes
                    for moulding tongue
To serve   6–8

You will need

1 ox tongue, about 4 lb., salted by the butcher
6 peppercorns
1 tablespoon vinegar
¼ pint (U.S. ⅝ cup) jellied stock, see recipe

Pressed ox tongue

Soak tongue in cold water for an hour, then rinse well and cut away excess fat and large gristly pipes around root.

Put tongue in a pan with cold water to well cover it, add peppercorns and vinegar.

Bring to boil, remove scum and simmer until tender when tested with carving fork. A tongue of this weight will take about 2½–3 hours.

When done, take up tongue and while still hot, remove skin.

Trim root end and underside neatly being careful to remove any small bones which should drop out easily if tongue is well done.

Press tongue into a soufflé dish or cake tin that is a tight fit for it. The thick part should be put to one side of the mould and the tip of tongue twisted round it. Fill in the hollow in centre and any crevices, with pieces of lean meat removed when tidying underside of tongue. Then pour in jellied stock, slowly so that it seeps right down into bottom of the mould and into any crevices and around the sides. The jellied stock is made by dissolving ¼ oz. powdered gelatine in ¼ pint (U.S. ⅝ cup) stock in which the tongue was boiled. Put a double circle of aluminium foil on top of the tongue and weight it with heavy weights resting on the tongue.

Leave until quite cold, then turn out onto serving dish, there will be a layer of delicious jelly around sides and bottom of tongue.

Slice very thinly and serve garnished with lettuce, tomato halves, sprigs of parsley and watercress.

SCOTCH EGGS

Preparation time 30–35 minutes
Cooking time   10–15 minutes
To serve   4

You will need

4 hard-boiled eggs
1 small onion, grated
8 oz. sausage meat
1 teaspoon chopped parsley
½ teaspoon mixed herbs
¼ teaspoon salt
good dash pepper
2 oz. fine breadcrumbs
1 small egg, beaten
1 tablespoon flour
lard for deep frying

Remove shells from eggs. Add grated onion to sausage meat; mix well, add parsley, herbs, salt and pepper, and breadcrumbs. Stir till well blended, then work the beaten egg into the mixture. Divide into four; flatten into round cakes with floured hands. Roll the eggs in flour, then encase them in sausage meat, pressing it firmly on, and making sure there are no cracks. Drop into hot fat to cover them and fry until crisp and brown, about 10 minutes. Take up with draining spoon and drain on absorbent paper. Serve hot, or cold with salad.

Scotch eggs

Cauliflower cheese

CAULIFLOWER CHEESE

Preparation time 20 minutes
Cooking time 25–30 minutes, including sauce
To serve 4

You will need

1 medium-sized cauliflower

FOR THE SAUCE

1 oz. butter
1 oz. plain flour
½ pint (U.S. 1¼ cups) milk
or milk and cauliflower water
½ level teaspoon salt
1 level teaspoon made mustard
pinch nutmeg
3 oz. Cheddar cheese, grated

Soak cauliflower in cold water for about 15 minutes, then break into flowerets. Cook in a little boiling salted water in a covered pan until tender and arrange neatly in buttered scallop shells or a fireproof dish.

TO MAKE CHEESE SAUCE

Melt the butter, add flour and cook for one minute. Remove from heat and add liquid gradually. Bring to the boil stirring well. Cook for a minute, remove from the heat, add the seasonings and grated cheese, and stir until cheese has melted. Coat the cauliflower with the cheese sauce. Serve hot.

BAKED STUFFED ONIONS

Preparation time 30 minutes
Cooking time 1¼ hours
To serve 4

You will need

4 large onions
1 oz. fat *or* dripping for frying
1 sheep's kidney
3 oz. pork sausage meat
2 tablespoons fresh breadcrumbs
1 egg yolk
salt and pepper
½ pint (U.S. 1¼ cups) onion stock thickened with
1 heaped teaspoon flour

Peel onions, boil in salted water for 10–15 minutes. Remove from water and drain thoroughly. Ease out centres from the onions. Finely chop the centres, then fry in a little fat or dripping for about 5 minutes. Remove pan from heat, add prepared chopped kidney, sausage meat and crumbs. Mix thoroughly, beat in egg yolk and season to taste. Pack stuffing into onions. Place in a shallow, lightly greased fireproof dish, pour thickened stock in. Bake in a slow oven (310°F. or Gas Mark 2), for 1 hour or till onion is tender. Baste once or twice during cooking. Stuffing for marrow, see page 62, can also be used for stuffed onions. Bake for 1 hour.

Baked stuffed onions

VARIATIONS

STUFFED TOMATOES

Do not pre-cook tomatoes. Cut ½-inch from the stalk ends of 4–6 large tomatoes.
Scoop out the centres and add the pulp to the stuffing mixture.
Use 1 small chopped onion in place of the onion taken from centres of onions.
Use stock made from a beef cube.

STUFFED PEPPERS

Remove the seeds and proceed as for onions.

PRESSED BRISKET OF BEEF

(Illustrated in colour on page 19)

Preparation time 20 minutes, after soaking meat
Cooking time 3 hours, including pressing meat
To serve 6–8

You will need

4–5 lb. salted brisket of beef
1 large onion
1 large carrot
2 bay leaves
1 dozen peppercorns
2 tablespoons vinegar
1 pint (U.S. 1¼ cups) aspic jelly, made from aspic jelly crystals

The butcher will salt the meat for you, but give him 3 day's notice in case he has to do it specially. Soak it 1½–2 hours, then rinse it and place in pan with water to cover, adding the peeled and roughly cut up onion and carrot, bay leaves, peppercorns and vinegar, no salt. Simmer, very gently 2½–3 hours, or until meat is tender when tested. Remove any bones. (The butcher would bone the meat for you, but it keeps a better shape if cooked with the bones in.) Press the meat into a square or oblong tin that is a tight fit for it. Cover meat with a board, or two or three sheets of aluminium foil and put weights on top, evenly distributed, and leave until quite cold.
Turn out meat on to a shallow dish when cold. Use stock from boiling the beef when making the aspic jelly. When jelly is on the point of setting, spoon

Baked potatoes stuffed with plaice

it over the beef. Leave to set, then cover with a second coat of jelly. Transfer to serving dish and leave until quite set.

BAKED POTATOES STUFFED WITH PLAICE

Preparation time 25–30 minutes
Cooking time 1½ hours
To serve 4

You will need

8 large potatoes
½ pint (U.S. 1¼ cups) shrimps, peeled
½ pint (U.S. 1¼ cups) cheese sauce, see page 148
salt and pepper
8 small steamed fillets plaice
sprigs parsley, to garnish

Bake potatoes in their jackets (425°F. or Gas Mark 7), for approximately 1–1½ hours. Cut a slice off the top lengthwise, scoop out the pulp and mix with the shrimps and two-thirds of the sauce and seasoning; return to the skins. Put a rolled fillet of plaice on each potato and coat with the remainder of the sauce. Reheat and serve garnished with parsley.

STEAK, KIDNEY AND MUSHROOM PIE

(Illustrated in colour on opposite page)

Preparation time 1 hour, including pastry
Cooking time   1½ hours
To serve   4–6

You will need

1½ lb. stewing steak
8 oz. ox kidney *or* 3 sheep's kidneys
1 teaspoon salt
½ teaspoon pepper
1 tablespoon flour
1 medium-sized onion
4 oz. mushrooms
¼ pint (U.S. ⅝ cup) stock *or* water
10 oz. rough puff pastry, see page 78

Wipe and cut steak into strips, 2-inches by 3-inches. Remove, core and skin kidney, and cut into small pieces. Add salt and pepper to flour and toss steak and kidney in it until coated all over. Roll each piece of kidney in a piece of steak. Peel and chop onion, wipe the mushrooms and cut in slices. Put a pie funnel in the centre of the dish, fill up with meat, sprinkling the onion and mushrooms among it, add the stock or water.
Roll out pastry thinly; cut off a strip about 1-inch wide. Dampen this strip and put it round rim of dish, pressing it down firmly. Dampen top of strip of pastry. Put on lid of pastry, avoiding stretching it. Press edges well together, then trim them. Knock them up making cuts about 1-inch apart all round.

Cut out leaves from pastry trimmings. Dampen these and arrange on top of pie. Brush with beaten egg and prick with a fork. Bake in hot oven (425°F. or Gas Mark 7), for 15 minutes, then lower heat to (350°F. or Gas Mark 4) and place pie lower in the oven. Cover with paper and bake for a further 1¼ hours.

BACON STOVIES (SCOTTISH)

Preparation time 20–25 minutes
Cooking time   1 hour
To serve   4

You will need

¾ lb. bacon, forehock, collar *or* streaky
1½ lb. peeled potatoes
4 oz. onions
½ teaspoon ground black pepper
½ teaspoon salt
¼ pint (U.S. ⅝ cup) milk
little lard *or* bacon fat

Cut the bacon into small pieces, removing rind. Slice potatoes and onions finely. Grease a casserole and arrange potatoes, bacon and onions in layers, seasoning well. Finish with a layer of potatoes. Pour over the milk. Dot with a little fat and cover tightly. Cook either in a moderate oven (350°F. or Gas Mark 4), or on the top of the stove for approximately 1 hour.

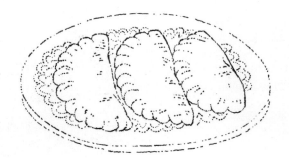

Cornish pasties; steak, kidney and mushroom pie; liver and bacon hot-pot with forcemeat balls

Deep rhubarb pie

PASTRY, SAVOURY AND SWEET

Britain could well be called 'The Land of Puddings, Pasties and Pies'. There seems to be no end to the variety; many counties and towns have their special pudding or pie. There is little doubt that from the earliest days pastry in some form was made, starting with a simple mixture of flour and water to form a covering for meat or bird to keep the goodness in. In time, fat in some form or another was added, and often milk and eggs, making a rich mixture that was in many cases a more important part of the pudding or pie than the contents.

It was Dr Johnson who defined in his dictionary 'Pie — any crust with something in it'. He certainly helped to make the old 'Cheshire Cheese' his favourite eating house in Fleet Street, London, famous for its steak, kidney and mushroom pie. Today it is still one of the most popular tourist attractions in London.

The 'something' in the crust can be, besides steak and kidney, pork, veal, chicken, pigeon, game of any kind. The crust can be a simple short pastry or a rich, meltingly tender flaky or puff pastry.

The making of 'raised' pies is an art peculiar to England. The hot water crust is raised by hand around a jar; in old days if you were skilled, it was moulded with your fist inside, as a potter moulds clay into a vase. The pie, after filling, was then baked without mould or tin so that the pastry became a rich brown all over, firm, yet crisp to eat.

MAIN TYPES OF PASTRY

SHORT PASTRY

8 oz. self-raising flour, 4 oz. cooking fat, ¼ teaspoon salt, cold water.

Always half as much fat as flour. Sieve flour and salt into mixing bowl; rub in fat with finger tips until crumbly, lifting flour well up. Mix to a stiff paste, first with knife then with fingertips, with cold water; turn onto floured board and work lightly until quite smooth. Use at once.

FLAKY PASTRY

8 oz. plain flour, 6 oz. cooking fat or lard, ¼ teaspoon salt, squeeze lemon juice, cold water.
(Three-quarters as much fat as flour.)

Sieve flour and salt into bowl; divide fat into four. Rub one portion into flour; mix to elastic dough with lemon juice and water. Roll out into strip about 8-inches wide. Dot one portion of fat down two-thirds of pastry; fold portion without fat over on to fat spread portion, fold over top third of pastry, press open edges lightly together with rolling pin. Give one half turn so that open ends are facing you. Roll out into strip same size as before, and repeat the process until remaining two portions of fat are used.

Finally fold into three and set aside at least an hour before using.

PUFF PASTRY

8 oz. plain flour, 8 oz. butter or mixture of lard and butter, 1 teaspoon lemon juice, ¼ teaspoon salt, cold water. (Equal quantity of fat and flour.) Press fat into an oblong piece in corner of floured cloth. It should be soft but not oily. Rub a small piece, about 2 oz. into the sieved flour and salt. Mix with water and lemon juice to a smooth elastic consistency; work lightly on floured board for a few minutes. Roll out into a square. Put the oblong of fat in the middle and fold sides of pastry over it, making a parcel. Press lightly with rolling pin so that fat spreads evenly inside the pastry; try to prevent fat leaking. Roll pastry into an oblong, keeping rolling pin well floured. Fold in three, give a half turn, so open ends are facing you. Roll again into an oblong; fold and roll out as before. Set aside in a cold place for ½ hour. Fold and roll twice more and set aside; fold and roll twice, leave in cold place as long as possible.

ROUGH PUFF PASTRY

8 oz. plain flour, 6 oz. lard, ¼ teaspoon salt, squeeze lemon juice, cold water. (Three quarters as much fat as flour.) Cut the fat into the sieved flour and salt, chopping and mixing until the fat is in pieces, about the size of a walnut. Mix with lemon juice and water, first with a knife, then with the hand until a solid mass is formed. Use little water; pressure from the hand should be used to bind fat and flour together. Roll out in an oblong on floured board, fold in three, lifting pastry well up so air is trapped. Close open ends with rolling pin, give pastry a half turn. Roll and fold again three times; set aside for at least an hour or longer before use.

BISCUIT OR FLAN PASTRY

6 oz. plain flour, 3 oz. butter, 1 egg yolk, ¼ teaspoon salt, water to mix. (Half as much fat as flour.) Rub butter into sieved flour and salt; stir in egg yolk and lemon juice. Mix to stiff dough with water. Roll out and use at once. For sweet flans, add about 2 teaspoons sugar dissolved in a little of the water.

SUET PASTRY

8 oz. self-raising flour, ¼ teaspoon salt, 4 oz. finely shredded suet, cold water to mix. (Half as much fat as flour.)
Mix all dry ingredients, and mix to an elastic dough with cold water. Use at once.

HOT WATER CRUST

1 lb. flour, 5 oz. lard, ½ teaspoon salt, ½ pint (U.S. 1¼ cups) milk and water. (Slightly less than one third as much fat as flour.) Mix flour and salt. Bring lard and liquid to boiling point. Pour into flour gradually, mixing with wooden spoon until all flour is mixed in and smooth mass is formed. Leave until cool enough to handle, then turn onto floured board and knead for 10 minutes or so, adding more flour if the pastry seems sticky, but do not get it too hard. While the pastry is still warm it must be moulded, or 'raised'. Reserve about a third for the lid of the pie, then shape rest into a flattish ball. Press middle thinner with your fist, then place a jam jar, 2 lb. size, or tin in middle and work pastry up to the top. When top is reached, roll jar on its side; this will smooth the pastry and loosen it. Lift out jar; the pastry by this time will be quite cool and ready for filling. Roll out the smaller piece to fit top of pie. To get a golden finish to pies, brush over with beaten egg let down with a dash of water, before baking.

The raising of the pie is not as difficult as it sounds as the pastry is a heavy mixture and does not mind being handled roughly. If you don't feel like tackling it however, you can use a hinged pie tin, and line this with the pastry, or loose bottomed cake tin, but the tin must be removed towards the end of baking so that the pastry can brown. Raised pies are usually served cold.

Traditionally, meat pies are decorated with pastry leaves, circles or diamonds, using up the scraps of pastry left over from trimming the pie crust. Steak and kidney pie should have a 'rose' in the middle, though this need bear little resemblance to the flowers.

Fruit pies were not decorated, for the practical reason that in the days when baking day was a serious business and several sweet and savoury pies made, it was easy to distinguish them on the pastry shelf, savouries decorated, sweet plain.

TO BAKE PASTRY CASE BLIND

Line pie tin with pastry; prick well to expel air, press pastry well on bottom and sides of tin. Put sheet of paper in bottom, cover with dried peas or beans or crust of bread to prevent pastry rising; remove these when pastry shell is baked.

This method is used when the pastry case is to be filled with a pre-cooked filling or with canned or bottled fruit.

BEEF STEAK AND KIDNEY PUDDING

(Illustrated in colour on page 37)

Preparation time 35–40 minutes, including pastry
Cooking time 3½–4 hours
To serve 4—5

You will need

8 oz. suet pastry, see page 78
1½ lb. stewing steak *or* skirt of beef
6 oz. ox kidney
1 tablespoon flour
1 level teaspoon salt
¼ teaspoon pepper
1 small onion
¼ pint (U.S. ⅝ cup) stock *or* water

Grease a 2-pint basin. Roll out two thirds of pastry in a round to fit basin, pressing it well against the sides. Cut beef and kidney into small pieces, removing skin, gristle and core from the kidney. Mix flour, salt and pepper and toss beef and kidney in it. Put those in pastry lined basin, sprinkling the chopped onion among them. Add stock or water. Roll out remaining pastry to fit top of basin, dampen edge of pastry in basin, put lid of pastry on top, pressing edges well together. Cover with greased paper, then with a pudding cloth. Place in pan with boiling water to come half way up the basin, and steam for 3½–4 hours. Serve immediately straight from the basin, with a napkin folded around.

KENTISH CHICKEN PUDDING

Preparation time 25–30 minutes
Cooking time 2½–3 hours
To serve 4

You will need

8 oz. salt belly pork
8 oz. suet pastry, see page 78
4 small chicken joints *or* 12 oz. uncooked chicken meat
1 large onion, chopped
pepper and salt
1 heaped tablespoon chopped parsley

Kentish chicken pudding

Cut pork into 1-inch cubes. Put into pastry lined basin with chicken joints, onion, pepper salt and parsley. Fill three quarters of the way up basin with water and put on the pastry lid. Cover with greased greaseproof paper, and cloth. Steam for 2½–3 hours in a deep saucepan with water to come half way up basin.

SAUSAGE ROLLS

Preparation time 40 minutes, including pastry
Cooking time 25–30 minutes
To serve 4

You will need

6 oz. flaky *or* rough puff pastry, see pages 77, 78
8 oz. sausages
egg to glaze

Roll out the pastry to 8-inches by 12-inches. Neaten the edges and cut into 4-inch squares. Squeeze the sausage from the skins on to one side of each piece, leaving ½-inch uncovered all round. Dampen edges and fold over. Flake the edges and prick tops with a fork, or mark with two or three cuts. Glaze with egg. Bake in hot oven (400°F. or Gas Mark 6), for about 5 minutes, then reduce heat to moderate (350°F. or Gas Mark 4) and bake 20–25 minutes.

SHROPSHIRE FITCHETT PIE

Preparation time 35 minutes, including pastry
Cooking time 50 minutes
To serve 4

You will need

1 oz. lard *or* pork dripping
8 oz. streaky bacon, coarsely chopped
8 oz. onions, peeled and sliced
1 lb. cooking apples, peeled, cored and sliced
1 tablespoon black treacle
1 tablespoon hot water
8 oz. flaky pastry, see page 77
pepper and salt

Melt fat in a pan, add bacon and onions and fry gently till transparent. Fill a 1½-pint heatproof dish with alternate layers of apples, fried onions and bacon, seasoning each layer with salt and pepper, then add black treacle mixed with hot water. Cover pie with pastry. Brush with beaten egg and bake in centre of a hot oven (400°F. or Gas Mark 6), for 10 minutes, then in a moderate oven (350°F. or Gas Mark 4) for 40 minutes.

MELTON MOWBRAY PIE

(Illustrated in colour on page 19)

Preparation time 40–45 minutes, including pastry
Cooking time 2½–2¾ hours
To serve 6

You will need

½–¾ pint (U.S. 1¼–1⅞ cups) jellied stock
1½ lb. lean pork
Melton Mowbray seasoning, see below
1 lb. hot water crust pastry, see page 78

FOR SEASONING

1 oz. salt	
½ teaspoon pepper	
¼ teaspoon cayenne	mixed
¼ teaspoon ground mace	together
pinch ground ginger	
pinch dried sage and marjoram	

The jellied stock is best made from pig's trotters and trimmings of pork, simmered with seasoning and herbs until liquid is well reduced. Failing this, a little gelatine should be added to ordinary the white stock.

Cut the pork into small pieces, add seasoning and stir until evenly distributed. Fill up pastry case with meat; add a *little* cold stock. Trim off top edge of pastry, dampen edge and put on the top round. Nip the edges well together so they stand up well. Make a hole in the middle and decorate top with leaves of pastry, see page 78. Brush over with beaten egg. Tie two layers of greaseproof paper round pie and bake in hot oven (425°F. or Gas Mark 7), for 10–15 minutes. Then reduce heat to moderate (350°F. or Gas Mark 4) and bake 2–2½ hours. Then cool, and pour in melted jellied stock and leave until cold.

PIGEON PIE

Preparation time 1 hour, including pastry
Cooking time 2 hours
To serve 4–6

You will need

3–4 pigeons, according to size
8–10 oz. puff pastry, see page 78
1 shallot, chopped
8 oz. slice beef steak
salt and pepper
4 oz. mushrooms, chopped
1 slice raw bacon, chopped
stock

Cut each pigeon into 4 or more pieces according to size. Put necks and trimmings on to boil for stock. Line edges of pie dish with rolled out pastry. Put shallot in bottom of dish, then put in the steak, cut into squares. Season the pieces of pigeon with salt and pepper and pack them into the dish, sprinkle the mushrooms and chopped bacon among them. Half fill the dish with stock. Cover with pastry, decorate and finish as for steak and kidney pie, see page 74, baking 1½–2 hours. Before serving fill up pie with more stock, and it is usual to put the well cleansed feet of one pigeon in the centre of the pie, firmly fixing them nearly upright, just before serving.

BUCKS BACON BADGER

Preparation time 40–45 minutes, including pastry
Cooking time 2½ hours
To serve 4

You will need

6 oz. suet pastry, see page 78
8 oz. bacon
1 medium-sized potato
1 medium-sized onion
½ teaspoon powdered sage
pepper to taste

Roll out pastry to a round on floured board. Remove rinds and brown edges from bacon; chop bacon, potato and onion finely, mix with the sage and pepper. Pile the mixture in the middle of the pastry, dampen edges of pastry, gather them together over top of bacon mixture and seal securely. Tie loosely in a well-floured cloth, place in pan of fast boiling water and boil steadily 2½ hours, replenishing pan with more boiling water if necessary. Take up onto a hot dish, remove the cloth carefully and serve at once.

BAKEWELL TART

(Illustrated in colour on page 85)

Preparation time 30 minutes
Cooking time 30–35 minutes
To serve 4–5

You will need

6 oz. short pastry, see page 77
2 oz. butter
2 oz. castor sugar
1 egg
2 oz. ground almonds
few drops almond essence
strawberry jam

Line a shallow tart tin with the pastry. Cream the butter and sugar until fluffy, beat in the egg, add the almonds and a few drops essence and beat well. Spread a layer of jam over the pastry, then put the almond mixture on top. Bake in hot oven (425°F. or Gas Mark 7) about 30 minutes, until golden brown. Sprinkle with castor sugar.

APPLE PIE

Preparation time 25–30 minutes, including pastry
Cooking time 30–35 minutes
To serve 4–6

You will need

2 lb. cooking apples
8 oz. short pastry, see page 77
4 tablespoons Demerara sugar
4 cloves
little castor sugar

Peel, core and slice apples. Half fill pie dish with the apples, then sprinkle in sugar and cloves, then rest of fruit. Roll out pastry a little larger than the dish, cut off a strip and place this round the wetted rim of the dish. Moisten this, and put lid on top. Press edges securely together and mark with a fork, or pinch them up. Make one or two holes in top. Put into a hot oven (425°F. or Gas Mark 7), for the first 10 minutes, then lower heat to (375°F. or Gas Mark 5) and bake for another 20–25 minutes. A few minutes before the pie is done, take it from the oven, brush over quickly with white of egg and sprinkle with castor sugar. Return to oven to finish baking.

Small stars may be cut out from the remaining pastry and used to decorate the pie as pictured in the photograph.

Apple pie

Cherry meringue pie

CHERRY MERINGUE PIE

Preparation time 1 hour, including pastry
Cooking time 30 minutes
To serve 4–6

You will need

1 7-inch–8-inch short pastry case baked blind,
 see page 78
1 lb. red cherries
½ pint (U.S. 1¼ cups) water
3–4 oz. sugar
few drops red colouring
juice 1 lemon
1 oz. fine semolina
3 egg yolks
½ teaspoon almond essence
2 oz. sugar

TO MAKE TOPPING

3 egg whites
pinch salt
5 oz. castor sugar

Stone and halve half the cherries. Stew cherries
with water and sugar 10 minutes, strain and add
red colouring if necessary. Add lemon juice and
water to make ¾ pint (U.S. 1⅞ cups) syrup. Heat
and sprinkle in semolina. Cook, stirring, until sauce
comes to the boil and thickens. Simmer gently for
2 minutes. Remove from heat.
Stir in the egg yolks, almond essence, sugar and
the halved cherries.
Cool slightly then turn into pastry case.

FOR MERINGUE TOPPING

Whisk egg whites and salt until stiff. Add 4 oz.
of the sugar and beat hard till meringue in shiny
and stiff and stands in firm peaks. Fold in rest
of sugar. Arrange in a thick border round the
edge of the pie, leaving the centre hollow. Bake
in a moderately hot oven (400°F. or Gas Mark 6),
for 4–5 minutes or till meringue is lightly topped
with gold. Pile up the centre with whole cherries.
Serve cold.

DEEP RHUBARB PIE

(Illustrated in colour on page 76)

Preparation time 40 minutes
Cooking time 20 minutes
To serve 4–6

You will need

flaky pastry using 12 oz. flour 8 oz. fat
 see page 77
2 lb. rhubarb, after removing leaves and stalk
 ends
4 oz. Demerara sugar
4 tablespoons warm water
2 1-inch strips lemon peel

Roll out pastry ¼-inch thick, keeping it to the
shape of pie dish only a little larger. Cut rhubarb
into 1–1½-inch pieces. Stand pie dish on pastry
and with a sharp knife cut it out a little larger
than pie dish, leaving a strip about 1-inch wide
to go round the rim of the dish. Dampen rim of
pie dish and put on 1-inch wide strip of pastry,
pressing it firmly. Stand a pie funnel in centre
of dish and put in half the rhubarb. Sprinkle in
the sugar, add warm water and remaining rhubarb.
Put the pieces of lemon peel at either end of the
dish. Dampen pastry rim and put on lid of pastry,
taking care not to stretch it. Press the two edges
of pastry together securely. Then with a pointed
knife held upright, mark the edge of the pie with
short cuts about ¾-inches apart. Brush over the
top of pie with a little milk. Make two cuts in
pastry for steam to escape. Bake in middle of hot
oven (425°F. or Gas Mark 7), for 15–20 minutes.
After about 10 minutes cover pie with sheet of
paper for remaining time. Sprinkle with castor
sugar and serve with cream.

Old English treacle tart

CUMBERLAND RUM NICKY

Preparation time 35–40 minutes
Cooking time 20–25 minutes
To serve 4

You will need

6 oz. short pastry, see page 78
8 oz. best stoned dates, chopped
4 oz. preserved ginger, chopped
2 oz. butter
1 oz. castor sugar
1 tablespoon rum

Divide pastry in half, roll out into rounds. Line a shallow pie dish with one round, pressing it well down and round the edge of pie dish. Prick the bottom well.
Put a layer of dates on pastry, then cover with ginger. Blend butter with sugar and half the rum, working it until it is a smooth paste.
Dot this all over the ginger in small pieces. Sprinkle with remaining rum. Dampen edges of pastry, put second round on top, pressing the edges well together. Prick the top. Decorate edges with a fork. Bake in a hot oven (425°F. or Gas Mark 7), for 20–25 minutes until pastry is well browned. This tart keeps well in an air tight tin.
Serve hot or cold with cream.

OLD ENGLISH TREACLE TART

Preparation time 20–25 minutes
Cooking time 15–20 minutes
To serve 4

You will need

4–6 oz. short pastry, see page 77
2 oz. breadcrumbs
rind and juice ½ lemon
small pinch ground ginger
4 tablespoons light treacle

Roll out the pastry thinly, line a shallow tart plate with it. Flute the edges. Mix the breadcrumbs with the lemon rind, juice and the ginger; spread this mixture over the pastry. Soften treacle, and dribble it evenly over breadcrumbs. Bake in a hot oven (425°F. or Gas Mark 7), for 15–20 minutes.

Note

If liked the tart can be decorated with pastry strips, before baking.

YORKSHIRE MINT PASTIES

Preparation time 30–35 minutes
Cooking time 20 minutes
To serve 4–5

You will need

6 oz. short pastry, see page 77
4 oz. currants
2 oz. soft brown sugar
1 oz. butter, melted
2 tablespoons fresh mint, finely chopped
grated rind ½ lemon
little milk

Roll out pastry thinly. Cut into circles, using a pan lid or saucer about 6-inches across. Mix together remaining ingredients except milk for the filling and place one half on each circle. Dampen the edges and fold over uncovered part of pastry and seal the edges firmly and crimp them. Brush over with milk. Bake in a moderately hot oven (400°F. or Gas Mark 6), for about 20 minutes, or until it is a golden brown.

WEST RIDING TART

Preparation time 35–40 minutes
Cooking time 1 hour 10 minutes
To serve 4–5

You will need

6 oz. short pastry, see page 77
jam
4 oz. flour
1 oz. cake crumbs
pinch salt
4 oz. butter
5 oz. castor sugar
2 eggs
½ teaspoons grated lemon rind
little milk

Roll out the pastry into a long strip to fit the sides of a deep pie dish. Trim the edges, dampen, and decorate with a narrow strip of pastry placed on top of the rim of pastry in the dish, and nipped up into peaks. Cover bottom of dish with jam. Mix flour, cake crumbs and salt. Cream butter and sugar together. Beat each egg separately and add to the creamed mixture. Beat for 5 minutes after adding second egg. Then fold in flour mixture, adding the lemon rind and a little milk to make a soft consistency. Spread this mixture over the jam. Bake in a hot oven (425°F. or Gas Mark 7), for 10 minutes to set the pastry, then reduce the heat to moderate (350°F. or Gas Mark 4) and bake for another ¾–1 hour.

MAIDS OF HONOUR (RICHMOND, SURREY)

(Illustrated in colour on opposite page)

Preparation time 40 minutes, including pastry
Cooking time 25 minute
To make 12 tarts

You will need

6 oz. puff pastry, see page 78
2 oz. curd cheese
1½ oz. butter
1 egg
1 dessertspoon brandy
2 oz. castor sugar
1 oz. ground almonds
grated rind and juice ½ lemon
few drops almond essence
¼ teaspoon grated nutmeg
little raspberry jam

Line 12 patty tins with the pastry. Squeeze cheese in cloth to dry it; beat cheese and butter together. Beat egg and brandy in separate bowl, add sugar, beat well, add ground almonds, lemon rind and juice, essence and nutmeg. Mix with the cheese and butter mixture and beat well. Put about ½ teaspoon of jam in each patty tin; cover with the mixture. Bake in hot oven (425°F. or Gas Mark 7), for 20–25 minutes

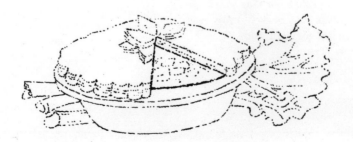

Bakewell tart; Yorkshire curd cheese tart; maids of honour

Queen of puddings

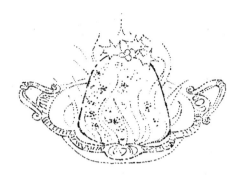

HOT PUDDINGS AND PANCAKES

There is something essentially British about sweet hot puddings. Let other countries have their desserts, gâteaux, soufflés, bombes glacés to finish off a meal, but the pudding belongs to Britain. Perhaps it is something to do with our climate. In the past it was considered a great help in keeping out the cold to eat filling, hot puddings. An interesting thing about our puddings is the way in which, in many of them, cake or bread, jam or syrup, dried or glacé fruits or nuts, the last drop of wine in the bottle, can be used up in making them.

It is a great convenience too, that many of our puddings are steamed, so that it is possible to leave them simmering gently for up to two hours or more while we go out. If you *do* go out and leave a pudding steaming, be sure that there is enough water in the pan for it not to simmer dry before you get back. Have a pan large enough to comfortably hold the pudding. If you have to add more water, add *boiling* water so that the cooking is not interrupted.

If you have to turn out a steamed pudding before you sit down for the main course, keep it covered with its basin, on a plate, standing over a pan of boiling water. It is better, really, to wait until the first course is finished before turning out the steamed pudding.

QUEEN OF PUDDINGS

(Illustrated in colour on opposite page)

Preparation time 50 minutes, including meringue
Cooking time 30–45 minutes
To serve 4–6

You will need

1 pint (U.S. 2½ cups) milk
6 oz. sponge cake *or* Madeira cake crumbs
1 liqueur glass brandy *or* Madeira wine
grated rind 2 lemons
2 oz. butter
6 oz. castor sugar
4 eggs
3–4 tablespoons strawberry jam
glacé cherries and angelica, for decoration

Warm milk and pour it over cake crumbs in mixing bowl and leave for ½ hour or long enough to soak crumbs. Add brandy or Madeira, grated lemon rind, and mix well. Mix in the softened butter and 2 oz. sugar. Separate egg yolks from whites, beat yolks into cake crumb mixture. When mixture is light and smooth pour it into a deep, well buttered pie dish. Bake in moderate oven (350°F. or Gas Mark 4), until set, 30–40 minutes. Spread the jam on top. Whip egg whites until beginning to stiffen, then add 2 oz. of remaining sugar and whip again until whites stand up in peaks, then lightly stir in remaining sugar. Pile this meringue on top of pudding, taking it well to the rim of the dish, so all jam is covered. Return to a cool oven (310°F. or Gas Mark 2) until meringue is set and lightly browned, 20–25 minutes. Decorate.

Chocolate sponge pudding

CHOCOLATE SPONGE PUDDING

Preparation time 25 minutes
Cooking time 2–2½ hours
To serve 4–5

You will need

6 oz. self-raising flour
2 oz. sweetened chocolate powder
¼ teaspoon salt
3 oz. best margarine
1 tablespoon sugar
1 egg
about 2 tablespoons milk
chocolate sauce, see below

FOR THE SAUCE

2 tablespoons plain chocolate, grated
1 tablespoon icing sugar, sieved
½ pint (U.S. 1¼ cups) milk
1 rounded tablespoon cornflour
½ teaspoon vanilla essence
½ oz. butter

Sieve flour, chocolate powder and salt together into mixing bowl. Cream margarine and sugar together; beat egg, add to creamed mixture. Beat 2–3 minutes. Stir in dry mixture, adding milk a little at a time until a softly dropping consistency is formed. Turn into greased pudding basin, to half fill it, cover with greased paper and piece of aluminium foil twisted securely over rim of basin. Stand in saucepan with boiling water to come half way up basin, and steam 2–2½ hours; add more

boiling water if first evaporates. Serve with hot chocolate sauce.

TO MAKE SAUCE

Mix chocolate and sugar to a paste with a little warm milk, then add rest of milk. Stir over low heat until boiling. Add the cornflour mixed to a paste with a little water; simmer 2 minutes. Add the vanilla essence and the butter. Stir until butter is well mixed.

CHRISTMAS PLUM PUDDING

(Illustrated in colour on page 134)

Preparation time 1–1½ hours, plus
overnight soaking
Cooking time 7 hours
To serve 6–8

You will need

8 oz. flour
1 level teaspoon salt
1 nutmeg, grated
½ teaspoon mixed cake spice
½ teaspoon powdered cinnamon
8 oz. fine white breadcrumbs
12 oz. shredded suet
8 oz. soft brown sugar
grated rind 1 lemon and 1 orange
12 oz. currants
12 oz. sultanas
12 oz. raisins
8 oz. chopped mixed candied peel
2 oz. blanched almonds, chopped
1 large carrot, grated
1 tablespoon black treacle
6 eggs
juice 1 orange and 1 lemon
2 tablespoons brandy
2 tablespoons rum
¼ pint (U.S. ⅝ cup) milk, approximately

Sieve flour, salt and spices together in a large mixing bowl. Add breadcrumbs, suet, sugar, grated lemon and orange rinds. Add prepared fruit, peel and almonds. Mix thoroughly then add grated carrot and stir it well in. Warm treacle to liquefy it and stir it into the mixture. Add eggs one at a time, mixing thoroughly. Then add orange and lemon juice and the brandy and rum; stir well. The mixture should be quite stiff but if it is very difficult to stir add a little milk. Leave the pudding mixture covered in a cool place overnight, then give it another thorough stirring. Put into two 2-pint basins, well greased; the basins should be two thirds full. Cover with greased paper and a pudding cloth, boil steadily for 7 hours in water to come almost to the rim of the basins, replenishing with boiling water if necessary during the cooking. Remove the puddings from the water when done. Take off the cloth and paper and leave until quite cold. Then cover with fresh paper and cloth and store in a cool cupboard until needed. Boil 2½–3 hours when required for eating. Serve with hard sauce or brandy butter.

HARD SAUCE

4 oz. butter
2 oz. castor sugar
1 oz. ground almonds
1 tablespoon sherry
2 tablespoons brandy

Cream butter and sugar together until quite smooth. Press the lumps out of the ground almonds and add this gradually to the creamed mixture. Then add sherry and brandy slowly and mix well. Chill before serving.

BRANDY BUTTER

4 oz. butter
5 oz. icing sugar, sieved
3 tablespoons brandy

Cream butter and icing sugar, then gradually beat in the brandy. Pack the mixture in a glass dish and chill before using.

SPICED APPLE DUMPLINGS

Preparation time 30 minutes
Cooking time   25–30 minutes
To serve   4–6

You will need

12 oz. short pastry, see page 77
6 medium-sized cooking apples
2 oz. brown sugar
½ teaspoon mixed cake spice
12 cloves

Roll out pastry thinly; cut into 6 squares, approximately 5-inches square. Peel and core apples, put each in the centre of a pastry square. Mix the sugar and spice and fill the cavities of apples with it. Stick 2 cloves in the sides of the apples, one each side. Dampen edges of pastry. Pull the corners of the squares up to the top of the apples; press the edges firmly together. Decorate tops with leaves made from scraps of pastry. Brush over with egg wash. Bake in hot oven (425°F. or Gas Mark 7), for 25–30 minutes.

SPOTTED DOG

Preparation time 25 minutes
Cooking time   2–2½ hours
To serve   4–6

You will need

8 oz. suet pastry, see page 78
3–4 oz. currants

Make the pastry, adding the currants before the water. Form into a roll. Roll in a floured cloth. Place on a rack in a saucepan of boiling water. Boil for 2–2½ hours. Or the pudding can be steamed over a pan of boiling water, allowing 3 hours. Serve with sweet white sauce, see page 149, or a dab of butter and sprinkling of sugar.

Spotted dog

JAM LAYER PUDDING (UPSTAIRS PUDDING)

(Illustrated in colour on page 95)

Preparation time 25–30 minutes
Cooking time 2–2½ hours
To serve 4–6

You will need

12 oz. suet pastry, see page 78
12 oz. jam, any kind

Well grease a 1½–2-pint pudding basin. Put a dessertspoon of jam in the bottom. Roll out pastry about ⅛-inch thickness. With a sharp pointed knife cut out a circle to fit bottom of the basin, and place it on top of jam. Cover this round of pastry with a layer of jam. Cover with a slightly larger round of pastry and then add another layer of jam. Continue in this way until all the pastry it used up, making sure the last layer is pastry. There will be 5–6 layers in all, including the top layer. Do not worry if the layers do not fit exactly against the sides of basin; in cooking they will rise and spread evenly. Sprinkle top of pudding with flour; cover with a sheet of waxed paper, then with pudding cloth or foil taken well over the rim of the basin. Stand basin in a pan with boiling water to reach half way up the side and boil steadily 2–2¼ hours. Allow to cool a little after taking the pudding up so that it will shrink a little from the sides, then run a knife round between basin and pudding and turn in out onto a hot plate. Serve immediately.

STEAMED APPLE PUDDING

Line a pudding dish with suet crust, see page 78 fill up with sliced apples, adding brown sugar to taste and one or two cloves. Do not add any water. Put on lid of pastry, and cover with greaseproof paper and cloth as described for steak and kidney pudding, see page 79.
Stand in pan with boiling water to come half-way up the basin.
Cook 2½–3 hours replenishing water as it evaporates with more boiling water.

Note

Other fruit could be used, but apple pudding is the most typical British one.

Jam sponge pudding

JAM SPONGE PUDDING

Preparation time 25 minutes
Cooking time 1½ hours
To serve 4

You will need

2 tablespoons jam
3 oz. butter
3 oz. castor sugar
2 small eggs
6 oz. flour
½ teaspoon baking powder
¼ teaspoon salt
grated rind 1 lemon
juice ½ lemon
little milk, if necessary

Well butter a 1½-pint pudding basin. Put jam in the bottom. Cream the butter and sugar until light, add beaten eggs one at a time, and beat until creamy. Sieve flour, baking powder and salt together, add lemon rind. Stir gradually into creamed mixture, add lemon juice and a little milk if necessary, to form a stiffly dropping consistency. Put in the basin, cover with aluminium foil twisted well over rim of basin, and steam for 1½ hours. Turn out and serve with extra melted jam as a sauce.

Note

In place of the jam, marmalade, lemon curd or honey could be used.

FIGGY PUDDING

Preparation time 25 minutes
Cooking time 2½–3 hours
To serve 4–6

You will need

6 oz. best dried figs
3 oz. blanched almonds, chopped
4 oz. self-raising flour
¼ teaspoon salt
4 oz. shredded suet
4 oz. fine white breadcrumbs
4 oz. sugar
¼ teaspoon grated nutmeg
¼ teaspoon grated cinnamon
grated rind ½ lemon
3 small eggs
1 tablespoon sherry *or* lemon juice
little milk, if necessary

Wash figs and chop them; mix with almonds. Sieve flour and salt. Add suet, breadcrumbs, sugar, figs and almonds and mix well. Then mix in the nutmeg, cinnamon and lemon rind. Mix with the beaten eggs and the sherry or lemon juice, adding a little milk if necessary, to form a softly dropping consistency. Put the mixture into a greased pudding basin filling it two thirds full, cover with greased paper and steam in pan with water coming half way up basin for 2½–3 hours. Turn out and serve with cream or egg custard, see page 98, flavoured with almond essence.

COFFEE RAISIN SPONGE

Preparation time 25–30 minutes
Cooking time 1½ hours
To serve 6

You will need

4 oz. butter
4 oz. castor sugar
2 eggs
6 oz. self-raising flour
3 oz. stoned raisins, chopped dates *or* mixed fruit
3 tablespoons coffee essence
1 tablespoon milk

Coffee raisin sponge

Well butter a 2-pint mould or basin.
Cream together butter and sugar until light and fluffy then beat in eggs a little at a time adding a tablespoon of the sieved flour with the last amount of egg.
Fold in remaining flour, raisins, coffee essence and milk. Turn into prepared mould and cover with a double layer of greased paper or foil.
Steam for 1½ hours. Turn out and serve with fresh cream and a sprinkling of Demerara sugar.

BREAD AND BUTTER PUDDING

Remove crusts from 4 slices of bread and butter; cut the slices into triangles.
Place alternate layers of bread and butter, butter side upwards and 1–2 tablespoons currants or sultanas to half fill a pie dish or ovenware glass dish or casserole.
Heat ¾ pint (U.S. 1⅞ cups) milk with 1 tablespoon sugar until sugar is melted, then add 2 beaten eggs and ¼ teaspoon vanilla essence.
Strain over the bread and fruit. Let it stand 30–40 minutes for bread to soak. Grate nutmeg on top, if liked. Bake in moderate oven (350°F. or Gas Mark 4), for about 1 hour, until golden brown and set.
Serve sprinkled with sugar.

PANCAKES AND FRITTERS

Pancakes or some form of batter puddings have been eaten in Britain from the very earliest times. In its simplest form the batter pudding was a mixture of batter, flour and milk, and flavourings, known as 'Hasty Pudding', being, as the name implies, quick to make and quick to cook. Really it was nothing more than a flavoured white sauce with butter, sugar and grated nutmeg or powdered cinnamon spread on the top while still boiling hot, so that butter, sugar and spices melted to make a delicious sauce.

The custom of serving pancakes on Shrove Tuesday began as a religious festival, this being the last feast day before the fast lasting until Easter Day. The pancakes were made from the last of the eggs, milk and butter left in the larder, and after that one supposes that a 'meagre' diet of bread, vegetables and water started on Ash Wednesday. The day was a holiday and fun was had by all, a custom still kept up, when we have 'pancake runs' in many places, and at least one famous public school (Westminster) has a pancake 'scramble', the pancakes being tossed over the rafters in the dining hall and scrambled for by the scholars, the aim being to grab the largest piece. A village in Bucks, Olney, has a pancake 'run' of housewives through the village, each carrying a frying pan with a pancake in it which must be tossed and caught 3 times during the running. A town in the U.S.A., Liberal, Kansas, holds a run at the same time, and there is friendly rivalry between the two teams to make the best time.

In Yorkshire and the North of England, Shrove Tuesday was known to us youngsters as 'Whip and Top' day. No one knows why, but suddenly every boy appears on the pavements with whip and top and the girls with battledore and shuttlecock. And of course lots of pancakes were eaten and still are though I doubt if the sophisticated youngsters of today keep up 'Whip and Top' day.

For frying pancakes pure lard or oil can be used. The pan should only be lightly coated; the best way is to melt the lard and quickly brush the bottom of the very hot pan over with it, or with oil, using a pastry brush.

The quickest way to turn a pancake is to toss it; really the movement is just a quick light flip from the wrist. Shake the pan in your right hand, after the first side of the pancake is cooked, until the side away from you slips down the rim of the frying pan, then give the pan a quick flip with a slightly forward and backward movement and the pancake will fall back into the pan on the other side. If you feel nervous about this you can turn the pancakes just as well with a palette knife or fish slice.

PLAIN PANCAKES

Preparation time 40 minutes
Cooking time   30 minutes
To serve   4–6

You will need

4 oz. plain flour
pinch salt
2 eggs
½ pint (U.S. 1¼ cups) milk
1 tablespoon cold water
melted lard *or* oil
sugar and lemon

Sieve flour and salt together into mixing bowl. Add eggs and stir into flour. Add half the milk slowly, stirring until a smooth paste is formed. The mixture must be quite smooth, before the remainder of the milk is added, slowly. Beat batter well, stand aside 30 minutes, then beat in the water. Put batter in a jug.

Make a 7–8-inch frying pan very hot, brush over with melted lard or oil. Pour in the batter slowly from the side of the pan, moving pan about so batter just covers the bottom of pan. Pancakes should be wafer thin.

When underside of pancake is a light golden brown turn or toss it and brown the second side. The whole process should not take more than 5–6 minutes. Brush the pan over with fat or oil for each pancake and be sure it is really hot. Serve with castor sugar and lemon juice, freshly squeezed from quartered lemons, and the pancake rolled up. This is often done at the table, but if preferred the pancakes can be sprinkled with sugar and lemon juice and rolled up as each one is fried.

The pancakes can be spread with jam, honey or lemon curd, in which case sugar will not be necessary.

Sausage and apple pancakes

SAUSAGE AND APPLE PANCAKES

Make batter as for plain pancakes. Cook 1 lb. sausages in a little fat until browned; keep hot. Make apple sauce, see page 149, and place in an ovenproof serving dish. Make pancakes wrap each sausage in a pancake and arrange on apple sauce; garnish with sprigs of parsley and serve hot.

VARIATIONS

CURRANT PANCAKES

Make batter as for plain pancakes, and sprinkle ½ teaspoon currants into each pancake as batter is poured into pan. Sprinkle with sugar and roll up.

SAVOURY PANCAKES

To the given quantity of plain pancake batter add 2 oz. minced cooked beef *or* pork, *or* chopped fried bacon, about 1 dessertspoon grated onion, pinch of herbs and salt, dash of pepper. Fry as for plain pancakes, but make a little thicker.

FRITTER BATTER

Preparation time 10–15 minutes, plus fruit preparation
Cooking time   5–8 minutes
To serve   4

You will need

4 oz. plain flour
pinch salt
1 tablespoon olive oil *or* melted lard
¼ pint (U.S. ⅝ cup) warm water less 1 tablespoon
white of 1 egg

Sieve flour and salt, pour the fat in the centre. Stir in warm water to make a thick coating consistency. Beat well until smooth. Beat egg white stiffly and fold into batter. Use at once.

Apple fritters

FRUIT FRITTERS

Apples should be peeled, cored and cut in slices; bananas, peeled and quartered; tinned fruits such as apricots, peaches, pineapple, should be well drained from juice. Have ready a pan of deep, hot fat. Place the fruit in the batter, lift out one by one with a skewer, allow surplus batter to drip off, then place in the pan. Do not crowd the pan. The pieces of fruit will soon rise to the top, turn them and allow to brown on underside, then turn again, and fry until golden brown all over. Drain well on kitchen paper, sprinkle with castor sugar and serve at once.

Note

A pinch of mixed spice or ground cinnamon may be added to the butter.

SAUCER PANCAKES

Preparation time 40 minutes
Cooking time 15 minutes
To serve 4–6

You will need

2 oz. plain flour
pinch salt
2 oz. butter
2 oz. castor sugar
2 eggs
¼ pint (U.S. ⅝ cup) milk
2 tablespoons water
jam

Sieve flour and salt into basin. Cream butter with sugar in mixing bowl, add beaten eggs, beat until light. Mix in half flour and salt. Then add half the milk and the water, slightly warmed; beat until smooth. Add remaining flour and when smooth, the remaining milk, and beat well. Leave for 30 minutes. Butter 6 large saucers or fruit dishes and two thirds fill them with the batter. Bake in a moderately hot oven (400°F. or Gas Mark 6), until well puffed up, then lower heat to (350°F. or Gas Mark 4), until firm and brown, about 10 minutes. Spread with jam, fold over and serve at once.

YORKSHIRE PUDDING

(Illustrated in colour on the jacket)

Yorkshire pudding is made from the same batter as used for pancakes. It's the simplest thing to make, yet it is known all over the world, and visitors to Britain insist that they must try it, and are often disappointed unless it is made by a Yorkshire woman. It is the traditional accompaniment to roast beef, though in its native county it is served as a separate course with beef gravy, preceding the beef, which is then served on the same plate. In days before the oven, the pudding was cooked in the drip pan underneath the meat suspended from the jack. It became rich with the hot drippings from the meat blending with the creamy mixture of egg, milk and flour. When the jack went out of use and meat was baked in the oven, the joint would be placed on a trivet four to five inches high, standing in the baking tin, and the batter poured into the tin 25–30 minutes before the meat was done. So the result was practically the same as with the roasting jack, a softish, creamy pudding rich with hot beef drippings.

Gradually it became more usual to bake the pudding in a separate tin, and the perfect pudding according to Yorkshire standards should be a well risen, puffy affair, crisp and brown top and bottom with a thin creamy layer inside, and baked in a pudding tin, not in small patty tins like popovers. It should be light as a soufflé, not the thick sticky slab so often presented under the name of Yorkshire pudding. Moreover, it should be served straight from the oven and from the tin in which it is baked; that is why restaurant Yorkshire pudding is rarely worth eating.

Make batter in the same proportions as given for pancakes, see page 92. 30 minutes before the beef is cooked, pour 2–3 tablespoons of its fat into a 10-inch square pudding tin, make sure it is sizzling hot and pour the batter in. Bake in the upper part of the hot oven 25–30 minutes; make sure there is enough overhead room for the pudding to rise. Serve at once, cut in squares, from the tin.

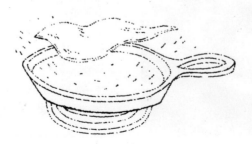

Jam layer pudding (upstairs pudding)

Strawberries and cream

DESSERTS

The soft berry fruit season begins in Britain in June and goes on until September and October in some parts. With the first strawberries in June we feel that summer has really arrived and we can forget about our filling, heat giving puddings; from now on fruit, fresh or cooked, will form our favourite desserts.

If you've never tasted our British strawberries, raspberries, black and red currants, gooseberries and cherries, to mention a few, you have a treat in store. Other countries may have bigger berries, but none to equal ours in their luscious juiciness and sweetness; perhaps it is some compensation for our long, rainy winter.

With the soft fruits season comes too the best season for our dairy produce, rich cream, butter, eggs and milk. We believe there is only one best way to eat strawberries, or raspberries, just as they are, with cream and castor sugar; the cream may be whipped, clotted, or thin.

STRAWBERRY MERINGUE PIE

Preparation time 25 minutes for the pastry case
Cooking time 15–25 minutes for the case and glaze, plus 10 minutes for meringue
To serve 4–6

You will need

6 oz. plain flour
1 oz. cornflour
pinch salt
1 dessertspoon castor sugar
3 oz. butter *or* butter and margarine mixed
2 egg yolks
1 tablespoon water
12 oz. strawberries
1 packet strawberry flavoured cornflour
3 tablespoons castor sugar
$\frac{3}{4}$ pint (U.S. $1\frac{7}{8}$ cups) milk
2 egg whites

Sieve flour, cornflour and salt together, add sugar and rub in fat until mixture resembles breadcrumbs. Beat egg yolks slightly, add the water and stir into dry mixture with a knife, then with the fingertips mix to a putty-like consistency, adding a little more water only if the mixture remains too crumbly. Roll out pastry, line an 8-inch tart tin and bake blind, see page 78, at (400°F. or Gas Mark 6), for 15 minutes, until golden brown. Leave to cool. Clean and mash strawberries, leaving few perfect ones for decoration. Mix flavoured cornflour and tablespoon sugar to a smooth paste with a little milk, boil rest of milk, pour it over cornflour stirring all the time. Pour all back into the pan and stir over low heat until boiling; simmer 2–3 minutes. Leave to cool then add mashed strawberries. When quite cold spread it in the pastry case. Whip egg whites with rotary whisk, adding remaining sugar gradually until stiff and dry. Pile this meringue on top of strawberry filling, taking it well up to the rim of pastry. Place in middle of moderate oven (350°F. — Gas Mark 4) for about 8 minutes. Decorate with strawberries.

Strawberry flan

Chocolate mousse

STRAWBERRY FLAN

Make a pastry case in the same way as for strawberry meringue pie; leave to go cold. Then cover
the bottom of the case with medium-sized strawberries placed pointed ends upwards; if the strawberries are large cut them in halves downwards
and place them cut sides downwards in the flan
case. Pour strawberry jelly made from 1 packet
jelly, cooled and on the point of setting, over the
strawberries, masking them and allowing it to fill
the spaces. Leave until jelly sets. Pipe ¼ pint (U.S.
⅝ cup) double cream, whipped, around the edge.

CHOCOLATE MOUSSE

Preparation time 35 minutes
Cooking time no cooking
To serve 4

You will need

4 oz. plain chocolate
1 tablespoon water
4 eggs
1 teaspoon vanilla *or* rum essence
1 dessertspoon sherry
little thick cream, whipped, stick of chocolate
   or chocolate finger biscuits, to decorate

Combine the broken up chocolate and water in the
top of double boiler or in basin standing in a pan

of boiling water. Stir until smooth, but do not
over heat. Separate eggs and add the yolks, one
by one, to the hot chocolate, beating well after
each addition. When last yolk is added, remove
pan or basin containing chocolate and yolks and
beat 2–3 minutes longer. Leave to cool while you
whip the egg whites stiffly. Add the flavouring to
the chocolate mixture, then fold in the stiff egg
whites, gently but thoroughly. Turn into 4 individual dishes and chill well before serving. Decorate
with whipped cream and chocolate bars or biscuits.

EGG CUSTARD

Preparation time 6–8 minutes
Cooking time 8–10 minutes
To serve 4

You will need

1 pint (U.S. 2½ cups) milk
4 teaspoons sugar
4 egg yolks
few drops vanilla essence

Warm milk sufficiently to dissolve the sugar. Beat
the egg yolks and stir into the warm milk and sugar.
Strain into a double saucepan, add flavouring and
stir, with boiling water in lower part of pan, until
custard thickens.

VARIATION

BAKED CUSTARD

Strain the egg and milk mixture into a greased pie dish, grate nutmeg on top, stand the dish in a baking tin of water and bake in a very moderate oven (335 °F. — Gas Mark 3) until set. An egg custard should never boil; the water in the baking tin prevents this.

STEAMED CUSTARD

Preparation time 10 minutes
Cooking time 45 minutes–1 hour
To serve 3–4

You will need

½ pint (U.S. 1¼ cups) milk
2 teaspoons sugar
3 eggs
1 teaspoon brandy *or* sherry

Warm milk to dissolve the sugar. Beat the eggs, stir in the warm milk and sugar. Add the brandy or sherry. Strain into a buttered basin or mould. Cover with buttered paper and steam gently 45 minutes — 1 hour, standing in a pan with water to come half way up mould. Water in pan must never actually boil; draw it away from direct heat.

CARAMEL CUSTARD

Preparation time 10 minutes
Cooking time 45 minutes–1 hour
To serve 3–4

You will need

3 oz. sugar
⅛ pint (U.S. scant ⅝ cup) water
½ pint (U.S. 1¼ cup) custard mixture
  as for steamed custard, see above

Dissolve sugar in water in small, thick pan. Boil rapidly, shaking the pan, do not stir until sugar changes colour; remove from heat. Sugar will now darken sufficiently in heat of pan. Pour at once, it soon hardens at this stage, into a hot, dry tin, or straight sided mould. Turn the mould around to

Caramel custard

coat sides and bottom. When cool and sticking to sides, pour in the prepared custard. Cover and steam as for steamed custard. To turn out, allow to cool slightly, ease edges from tin or mould and invert over plate. East out without shaking. The caramel will run over the pudding making a sauce.

JUNKET

Preparation time 5–6 minutes
Cooking time 5–6 minutes
To serve 4

You will need

1 pint (U.S. 2½ cups) new milk, unpasteurised
  if possible
1 dessertspoon castor sugar
1½ teaspoons rennet
grated nutmeg

Warm the milk to blood heat; test by dipping in the little finger. Temperature is just right if heat cannot be felt. Dissolve sugar in milk then stir in rennet.
Pour into a warm dish. Leave junket to set in a warm room. Grate nutmeg on top. For flavouring junkets add a few drops vanilla or almond essence after rennet is added. Five drops of peppermint essence gives an unusual refreshing flavour. Individual junkets can be made and, of course, set quicker.

Rich English trifle

RICH ENGLISH TRIFLE

Preparation time 1½–2 hours, allowing for jelly to set, whip cream and decoration
Cooking time no cooking
To serve 6–8

You will need

6 sponge cakes *or* equal amount of stale cake
4 oz. sponge finger biscuits
2 oz. ratafia biscuits
little strawberry *or* raspberry jam
2 wine glasses sherry *or* Madeira wine
1 packet jelly, flavour to match jam
1 banana
1 orange
4 oz. black grapes
4 oz. glacé cherries
crystallised orange and lemon slices
assorted glacé fruits
few silver cachous
2 oz. shelled walnuts
2 oz. blanched almonds

EGG CUSTARD

1½ pints (U.S. 3¾ cups) milk
2 tablespoons castor sugar
4 egg yolks
few drops vanilla essence
½ pint (U.S. 1¼ cups) thick cream, whipped

Cut sponge cakes or cake into slices, sandwich them together with jam. Arrange them in bottom of glass bowl. Pour the sherry or wine over them.

Leave to soak. Dissolve the jelly square. Arrange the sponge fingers upright around side of bowl, wetting them with a little jelly to help them stick. Pour remaining jelly over the soaked sponge cakes. Cover with chopped fresh fruit and chopped nuts, reserving some for top of trifle. Leave to set. Make the custard.

When it is cool but not stiff, pour it over contents of bowl, spreading evenly. When quite cold spread with cream. Decorate with glacé cherries, sliced glacé fruits, crystallised orange and lemon slices and seeded grapes. Pipe whipped cream around sides and between fruits; decorate with walnut halves, sliced blanched almonds and silver cachous. There is no hard and fast rule about the decoration of a trifle, or about the fruit that is put into it; small quantities of fruit, fruit salad, nuts, etc., not enough for anything else, can be used.

TO MAKE EGG CUSTARD

Warm the milk sufficiently to dissolve the sugar. Beat egg yolks and stir into milk and sugar. Strain into a double saucepan, add vanilla flavouring and stir, with boiling water in lower part of pan, until custard thickens.

SIMPLE SYLLABUB

(Illustrated in colour on the jacket)

Preparation time 25–30 minutes
Cooking time no cooking
To serve 4–6

You will need

4 oz. granulated sugar
1 grated nutmeg
grated rind 1 lemon
½ pint (U.S. 1¼ cups) sweet wine *or* cider
½ pint (U.S. 1¼ cups) sherry
1½ pints (U.S. 3¾ cups) new milk

Put the sugar, grated nutmeg, grated lemon rind, wine and sherry into a bowl and stir until sugar is dissolved. Make the milk lukewarm and put it into a teapot.
Pour from a height into the bowl until mixture is well frothed. Serve cold with a little whipped cream and ground cinnamon if liked.

Apricot soufflé omelette

Cherry sponge flan

APRICOT SOUFFLE OMELETTE

Preparation time 15–20 minutes
Cooking time 8–10 minutes
To serve 2–3

You will need

2 large eggs
1 dessertspoon castor sugar
½ oz. butter
8 oz. stewed apricots

Separate eggs. Add half an egg shell of water per egg, and the sugar to the yolks. Beat with a wooden spoon until creamy. Whisk whites until they stay in the basin when turned upside down. Fold the whites, gently, into the yolks. Meanwhile, put the butter in the omelette pan, place on heat and slowly get it hot, but not so hot as to burn the butter. Pour in the egg mixture. Cook until it is golden brown on the underside. Put the frying pan under a hot grill and lightly brown the omelette top. Run a spatula round the edge and slip the omelette on to a hot, serving dish. Place cooked apricots on half the omelette, with apricot syrup if liked, then fold the omelette in half. Serve immediately.

Note

Other fresh or cooked fruit can be used. If possible use a special omelette pan with a rounded join between sides and base; after use wipe the pan with tissue paper, avoid washing it.

CHERRY SPONGE FLAN

Preparation time 10–15 minutes
Cooking time 20–25 minutes
To serve 4–5

You will need

2 oz. best margarine
2 oz. castor sugar
few drops vanilla essence *or* grated rind ½ lemon
1 egg
2 oz. self-raising flour
2 teaspoons hot water
8 oz. stewed cherries

FOR THE GLAZE

1 level teaspoon cornflour
⅛ pint (U.S. scant ⅝ cup) sweetened fruit juice
thick cream, whipped, to decorate

Make flan as for Victoria sandwich cake, see page 141, and put mixture into lightly greased 6-inch sponge flan tin. Bake in a moderate oven (350°F. or Gas Mark 4), for 20–25 minutes. Turn out and cool on cake rack. Drain and stone cherries and fill centre of flan.

TO MAKE THE GLAZE

Blend cornflour in the fruit juice; bring to the boil and cook for several minutes, stirring all the time. Cool and pour over fruit. Decorate with whipped cream.

APPLE AND BLACKBERRY VOL-AU-VENT

Preparation time 30–40 minutes, pastry and case
Cooking time 15–25 minutes
To serve 4–6

You will need

8 oz. puff pastry, see page 78
little milk *or* egg white
1 14 oz. can apple and blackberry fruit filling
icing sugar

Roll out the pastry to a rectangle 9-inches by 6-inches. With a 2¾-inch pastry cutter, cut out 12 rounds. Place 6 on a baking sheet and brush around the edge of these with cold water. Cut a 1½-inch circle out of the remaining rounds and place the centre pieces on the baking sheet. Carefully place a pastry ring on top of each of the rounds already on the baking sheet. Brush the tops with a little milk or egg white.
Bake for about 15 minutes (425°F. or Gas Mark 7), until cooked. Meanwhile empty the can of apple and blackberry fruit filling into a small saucepan. Heat gently and place in each vol-au-vent. Dredge with icing sugar. Serve hot.

Note

Fresh stewed blackberries and apple may be used in season, but it should be sieved.

BLACKCURRANT FLUMMERY

Preparation time 15 minutes
Cooking time 25–30 minutes
To serve 4

You will need

1 lb. blackcurrants
1 pint (U.S. 2½ cups) water
1 dessertspoon cornflour
4 oz. castor sugar
2 teaspoons lemon juice
2 eggs

Stalk and wash the currants and stew gently in the water until tender, then sieve them.
Mix cornflour to a smooth paste with a tablespoon of the blackcurrant purée. Put rest of purée on to boil with the sugar. When boiling add the blended cornflour and the lemon juice and cook for 2 minutes stirring all the time to prevent sticking. Leave to cool. Separate the eggs, beat the yolks and add to cooled blackcurrant and cornflour mixture, mixing well. Whip egg whites to a stiff foam and fold into the mixture when cold. Pour into glass serving bowl; serve with cream or egg custard, see page 98.

BILBERRY AND BANANA SUNDAE

Preparation time 15 minutes
Cooking time no cooking
To serve 1

You will need

2 tablespoons vanilla ice cream, ready made
1 banana
2 tablespoons bilberries
1 tablespoon sugar
1 tablespoon thin cream

Put the ice cream in a tall glass. Slice half the banana and cover the ice cream with it; stand remaining half banana upright on top of sliced banana and ice cream. Clean the bilberries; sprinkle with sugar. Arrange them round the banana in centre of glass; pour cream over the top. This is a quickly made last minute sweet.

FRUIT FOOLS

In their simplest form, fruit fools are a mixture of sieved stewed fruit with custard; often today they are made with custard powder custard, but originally they were made with an enriched egg custard and whipped cream and were very good indeed. Gooseberry fool is the best known, though any soft fruit can be used. The fruit should be cooked in as little water as possible, if any; the secret of a good fool is to have the fruit and the custard the same consistency, so that they whip up into a fluffy cloud, not a thin, watery stew. Oven stewing is the best method so that the juice is extracted in slow, steady heat.

Gooseberry fool

GOOSEBERRY FOOL

Preparation time 20–30 minutes
Cooking time 30–40 minutes
To serve 4

You will need

1½ lb. green gooseberries
2 oz. butter
2 tablespoons sugar
1 pint (U.S. 2½ cups) egg custard, see page 98
4 tablespoons thick cream, whipped

Top and tail the berries, wash them and put them in a stew jar or casserole (reserving 4 for decoration) with only the water clinging to them. Cover closely and cook in a very moderate oven (335°F. or Gas Mark 3), until soft.
Rub through a sieve. While still hot beat in the butter and the sugar. Leave to go cold, fold in the cold custard. Put into individual dishes Place the cream in a piping bag fitted with a star tube and pipe a whirl of cream in the centre of each. Top with reserved gooseberries.

Bilberry and banana sundae

GOOSEBERRY TANSY

Top and tail and wash 1 lb. gooseberries, put them in a stew jar or casserole with 1 oz. butter and cook in a very moderate oven (335°F. or Gas Mark 3), until tender. Sieve through a coarse sieve into a saucepan or flameproof casserole. Place over low heat. Beat 2 eggs, add 2 tablespoons fine white breadcrumbs and 2 tablespoons castor sugar; add to the gooseberry pulp, and stir until the mixture thickens. Do not let it get too hot or the egg will curdle; it is really better to use a double saucepan. Turn out onto a hot dish and sprinkle with a little extra sugar.
Serve with raspberry or red currant jelly.

RASPBERRY AND RED CURRANT PUDDING

Preparation time 20–25 minutes
Cooking time 1–1¼ hours
To serve 4–6

You will need

8 oz. raspberries
4 oz. red currants
2 oz. granulated sugar
4 oz. butter *or* best margarine
3 oz. castor sugar
3 eggs
6 oz. self-raising flour
2–3 tablespoons milk

Pick over raspberries, remove stalks from currants and put fruit in a well buttered oven glass pie dish. Sprinkle with sugar. Beat the butter or margarine and sugar in mixing bowl until light and creamy; add one beaten egg, beat for a minute or so, gradually adding half the flour. Add remaining beaten egg, beat well, then stir in rest of flour. Add sufficient milk to make a fairly soft mixture that drops easily from the spoon. Spread mixture evenly over fruit. Bake in a moderate oven (350°F. or Gas Mark 4) for 1–1¼ hours until well risen and golden brown. Sprinkle with castor sugar just before serving; can be served hot or cold, with thin cream or pouring custard.

SUMMER PUDDING

Preparation time 30 minutes
Cooking time 10–15 minutes
To serve 4–6

You will need

8 oz. blackcurrants
8 oz. raspberries
4 oz. red currants
4 oz. sugar
½ packet raspberry jelly
6–8 slices buttered white bread

Stalk and clean fruit, and place in a pan (reserve a few raspberries for decoration) with the sugar; heat slowly to boiling point. Dissolve the jelly in ¼ pint (U.S. ⅝ cup) of hot juice and a little water if necessary to make up the ¼ pint (U. S. ⅝ cup); add this to the fruit.
Line a 1½-pint sized plain mould or pudding basin with bread, removing crusts and placing the buttered sides next to the basin. Cut the pieces if necessary so that they fit closely; keep back sufficient to cover top of basin. Fill the lined mould with fruits, reserving a little of the juice. Cover with a layer of buttered bread. Put a plate or saucer on top resting on the pudding and weight it lightly. Leave overnight in a cold place. Turn out on to serving dish. Liquify the left over juice if it has set hard, let it cool, then pour over top of pudding. Decorate with remaining raspberries.

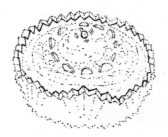

Summer pudding

OLD BRITISH PRESERVES
AND BOTTLING

In the days before the commercial manufacture of jams and jellies, pickles and chutneys, and before ships of every nation came to these shores filled with fruits and vegetables out of season, in this country, households had to depend on the domestic preservation of fruits and vegetables to see them through the winter.

The harvesting of fruits and vegetables in the gardens, fields and hedgerows, saw the housewife busy all day long with her pots and pans and the pleasant smell of boiling fruit, herbs, spices and vinegars filled the house. For what couldn't be eaten had to be pickled, potted or preserved in some manner; nothing must be wasted. With a well filled store cupboard the housewife could face the winter with an easy mind; there was always something to give a lift to the dullest meal even though she couldn't pop round the corner to the shops any time of day.

Today this is a most interesting branch of cookery and however good the manufacturer, there is something different about the home-made preserves.

FRUIT BOTTLING

The simplest way of bottling fruit is by the water bath method. Failing a special steriliser, a large saucepan, fish kettle, zinc bath or bucket with lid may be used. A false bottom must be placed in the vessel, pieces of wood laid crosswise, wire grid, straw or pads of newspaper. Jars must not touch; put newspaper between them. Use screw top jars with glass tops and rubber rings; see that these are sound; rubber rings should fit perfectly and be fully elastic. Plastic lined lids are new and very good. Fruit for bottling should be sound and just ripe; it can be bottled in plain water or syrup. Syrup is better as sugar is a preservative and helps to keep fruit a good colour. Use $\frac{1}{4}$–$\frac{1}{2}$ lb. sugar to 1 pint (U.S. $2\frac{1}{2}$ cups) water; put sugar and water into pan, allow sugar to dissolve, then boil 2 to 3 minutes. Leave to go cold before adding to fruit. If plain water is used, boil it first. Fruit should be graded for size to ensure even cooking. Pack jars tightly without crushing fruit; use spoon handle to work large, hard fruits into bottom of jars.

When jars are packed with fruit, fill up with boiled water or syrup until overflowing, put on rubber bands and glass tops, then put on screw bands loosely. Stand in pan with cold water to come well over shoulders of jars, place cover on pan. Heat very gently, taking $1\frac{1}{4}$–$1\frac{1}{2}$ hours to reach boiling point. Hold at this temperature 10–15 minutes. Remove jars from pan one at a time and tighten the screw bands immediately. Leave until quite cold. Next day remove screw bands and test for a good seal by lifting jars slightly, hold the lid; if this lid is loose fruit must be re-sterilised. If there is a good seal, replace screw band tightly and store jars.

PREPARING THE FRUIT

APPLES AND PEARS

These should be peeled, cored and halved and put straight into salted water to keep them white, 1 tablespoon to 2 pints (U.S. 5 cups) water. Drain and rinse well before using.

Pears can be bottled whole in syrup by a special method, see opposite.

CHERRIES

These can be stoned. It is worth the trouble if you are careful to catch all juice and add it to jars. Wash the fruit. The black and red varieties are best for bottling, as these retain their colour and flavour better than the white varieties.

GOOSEBERRIES

Top and tail, snipping away a little of the skin at each end to prevent skins wrinkling and to make sure syrup penetrates the fruit.

RHUBARB

Should be wiped with damp cloth and cut into 2–3-inch lengths; or if small jars are used, rhubarb can be cut into lengths same as height of jar and stood upright in the jars; it looks very attractive this way. Pour over it the hot syrup in which it is to be bottled and leave overnight before placing in jars; this improves flavour. Use only red rhubarb and cut away at least 1-inch from the leaf end, and of course remove root end.

APRICOTS

These bottle well. They are not usually peeled but halved and stoned; some of the stones can be cracked and the kernels added to the jars.

PEACHES

These should be peeled. Proceed as for apricots.

LARGE PLUMS

These are washed and halved and stoned; small plums, damsons, greengages, wash and keep whole.

BLACKBERRIES

Wash and drain well; use only firm ones. Small blackberries are too seedy to be worth while, but larger berries are useful for winter pies, with apples.

BLACK AND RED CURRANTS

Remove carefully from stalks; it is not really necessary to remove the brown blossom ends from the black currants.

RASPBERRIES AND LOGANBERRIES

Avoid washing; wipe gently in towel. Use only firm, sound berries. Raspberries sink a lot during bottling and must be sterilised very gently.

They can be sterilised in their own juice, with just a sprinkling of sugar added, but will sink in the jars.

STRAWBERRIES

These can be bottled but they are inclined to lose their colour.

If bottled in red currant juice, or red rhubarb juice they keep better colour.

PEARS PRESERVED IN SYRUP

(Illustrated in colour on page 114)

Preparation time 30 minutes
Cooking time 25–30 minutes
To yield 2 large jars

You will need

3 lb. granulated *or* loaf sugar
1 pint (U.S. 2½ cups) water
yellow rind and juice 3 lemons
1-inch piece root ginger
4 lb. ripe, firm pears

Put sugar, water, lemon rind and juice and ginger in an enamel pan and bring to the boil. Peel the pears, keeping on the stalk; if large, pears may be halved, but they are less likely to break if they are kept whole.

As each pear is prepared, put it into the boiling liquid. When all pears are in, cover pan closely and simmer very gently until pears are quite tender, 10–15 minutes, but not broken. Take them up carefully with perforated spoon and place in hot jars. Keep the pan boiling all the time you are doing this. As each jar is filled with pears, pour in the syrup over them and cover and screw jars down immediately.

Try to arrange the pears upright in the jars, without overcrowding them.

They are less likely to crush and lose their shape this way.

Ready for use within a few days.

BOTTLED WHOLE TOMATOES

(Illustrated in colour on page 114)

Choose firm, ripe tomatoes of equal size, about the size of a golf ball. Skin them by pouring boiling water over; then skins can be easily removed with a knife. Pack carefully into wide necked, scalded jars; do not force them in, but fill the jars comfortably. Sprinkle 1 teaspoon cooking salt and ½ teaspoon castor sugar into each 2 lb. jar. Fill up the jars with cold, boiled water, put caps on jars, and the screw bands loosely. Stand the jars in a pan with water to come up to necks of jars. Put lid on pan, and slowly raise the water to boiling point, taking 1½ hours; maintain at this temperature 20 minutes. Remove jars, and tighten the screw band as each jar is removed. Leave to go cold, tightening the screw band from time to time.

BRANDIED PEACHES

Preparation time 15–20 minutes
Cooking time. 25–30 minutes
To yield 21 lb. jars

You will need

1 lb. medium-sized peaches
12 oz. sugar
½ pint (U.S. 1¼ cups) water
brandy

Do not skin the peaches, but rub the fuzz off them with a cloth dipped in hot water. Boil sugar and water together for 8 minutes, without stirring. Add peaches, a few at a time, and cook until tender, about 5 minutes; if the peaches are not covered with syrup, spoon it over them. Remove peaches with perforated spoon and pack closely, but without crushing, into wide necked sterilised jars. Cook the syrup a little longer until thick, measure it and add an equal amount of brandy, bring to boiling point and pour over the peaches to the brim of the jars. Seal at once.

SPICED OR PICKLED PEACHES

Preparation time 30–40 minutes
Cooking time 30 minutes
To yield 3–4 small jars

You will need

2 lb. firm peaches
¼ pint (U.S. 1¼ cups) white wine vinegar
1 lb. granulated sugar
¼ oz. cloves
6-inch stick cinnamon
¼ oz. whole allspice

Dip the peaches in boiling water and remove skins by gently pressing them with the thumbs. Small or medium-sized peaches can be pickled whole but large ones should be split in halves. Boil vinegar, sugar and spices together; when boiling put in the peaches and simmer until tender, 5–8 minutes. Remove them with a perforated spoon and pack into heated jars; Boil sugar, vinegar and spices again until syrupy, about 8 minutes, then strain it into the jars. Cover and screw down immediately. Keep at least a week before using.

NOTES ON JAM MAKING

Fruit should be sound and under, rather than over ripe. Never use more water than is necessary; water will never set jam. Too long boiling to evaporate the water causes jam to be a bad colour. Use granulated, lump *or* preserving sugar. Heat the sugar before adding it to the jam, this hastens the dissolving and setting time. Fruit must *always* be thoroughly cooked before sugar is added; addition of sugar stops the tenderising process and jam will not set because pectin has not been sufficiently extracted. After adding sugar do not allow preserve to boil until sugar has dissolved; then boil quickly until set. Remove scum at end of cooking process; too frequent removal wastes jam. Allow jam to stand for a few minutes before potting; then stir before potting. Use scalded, hot jars. Cover at once with wax discs and screw top lids or leave until quite cold. *Never* cover while lukewarm.

HEDGEROW JAM

Preparation time 25–30 minutes
Cooking time 45–50 minutes
To yield 5–6 lb.

You will need

8 oz. rose hips
8 oz. hawthorn hips
8 oz. rowans
8 oz. sloes
1 lb. crab apples
1 lb. blackberries
1 lb. elderberries
4 oz. hazelnuts
sugar

Pick over the fruit for stalks, etc., then rinse it; simmer the hips, haws, rowans, sloes and chopped crab apples in water, to float them, until tender, about 15 minutes. Press through a sieve. Put pulp in pan with the blackberries, elderberries and chopped nuts. Simmer for 15 minutes, then measure. Add an equal measure of sugar, heat the sugar and add to the pulp, stir until sugar is dissolved without boiling, then boil up and simmer 15–20 minutes or until jam sets. Put into heated jars and tie down while hot.

SEEDLESS BLACKBERRY JAM

Preparation time 25–30 minutes
Cooking time 40–45 minutes
To yield 6–7 lb.

You will need

4 lb. blackberries
1¼ lb. sour apples
¾ pint (U.S. 1⅞ cups) water
loaf *or* preserving sugar

Pick over and wash blackberries. Stew over low heat with very little water added, until all juice is extracted and fruit is soft. Pass it through a sieve. Peel, core and cut up apples and stew in the water until reduced to pulp. Add blackberry pulp. Weigh and add equal weight of warmed sugar. Stir until sugar dissolves then boil steadily 20 minutes, or until setting point is reached.

Whole fruit strawberry jam

To weigh the pulp first weigh the vessel containing it, add the pulp, weigh again and subtract weight of vessel.

WHOLE FRUIT STRAWBERRY JAM

Preparation time 30 minutes
Cooking time 35–40 minutes
To yield 5–6 lb.

You will need

4 lb. strawberries
3½ lb. loaf sugar
¼ pint (U.S. ⅝ cup) water
¼ pint (U.S. ⅝ cup) red currant juice
juice 2 large lemons

Choose small, just ripe berries. Remove stalks and clean berries by rubbing gently in a tea towel. Avoid washing them; remove all damaged ones. Put sugar, water and red currant juice in preserving pan, stir over low heat until sugar dissolves, then boil steadily until syrupy, when tested on cold plate. Then add the strawberries and lemon juice and boil quickly for 10–15 minutes. Do not stir much lest you break the fruit, but skim well. Allow to cool in the pan for 15 minutes or so, then stir well, but gently and pot up into hot jars. Tie down when quite cold.

RHUBARB GINGER JAM

Preparation time 20 minutes
Cooking time 50 minutes
To yield 5–6 lb.

You will need

4 lb. red rhubarb
4 lb. sugar
4 large lemons
8 oz. crystallised ginger

Wash rhubarb and cut into 1-inch pieces. Place it in a jar or casserole with a quarter of the sugar, cover it and cook in a cool oven (310°F. or Gas Mark 2) until soft but not broken, 15–20 minutes. Then put the rhubarb in a preserving pan with rest of sugar and lemon juice and cut up ginger. Boil steadily until jam sets, about 30 minutes, and just before jam is finished add the grated rind of lemon. Put into hot jars and cover at once.

LEMON CURD

Preparation time 20 minutes
Cooking time 15 minutes
To yield 1 lb.

You will need

4 oz. butter
8 oz. granulated sugar
3 eggs
grated rind and juice 2 lemons

Melt butter in top part of a double saucepan, placed over low heat. Add sugar slowly and stir until well blended. Beat eggs and pour them gradually into the butter and sugar. Stir until mixture is light and creamy; do not allow it to get very hot. Grate the yellow peel from the lemons and add it to the mixture. Squeeze the juice from lemons and add it slowly stirring all the time. Place the pan over the lower part of double saucepan with boiling water in it, over low heat, and heat and stir until curd forms a film on back of spoon. Pour into a screw top jar.

SOME BRITISH MARMALADES

The traditional coarse cut bitter marmalade which is part of the British breakfast is made from Seville oranges, which are at their best during January and February. But marmalade can be made from any of the citrus fruits, sweet oranges, grapefruit and lemons. These fruits make a sweeter marmalade that is more suitable for tea time.

Though marmalade can be eaten within a few weeks of making it, the flavour improves with keeping, the longer the better. There is, in fact, one Scottish firm that sells 'vintage' marmalade, sold only after being matured in whisky casks! One way of having whisky with your breakfast.

COARSE CUT MARMALADE

Preparation time 1–1½ hours, plus overnight soaking
Cooking time 2½–2¾ hours
To yield 9–10 lb.

You will need

3 lb. Seville oranges
1 sweet orange
2 lemons
6 pints (U.S. 15 cups) water
pinch bicarbonate of soda
6 lb. Demerara sugar

Wash fruit, cut into quarters, remove loose pith Cut up fruit coarsely, or put through mincer, catching all juice and removing pips; put pips in separate basin; cover them with ½ pint (U.S. 1¼ cups) of the water. Cover chopped fruit with remaining water and soda; leave overnight. Transfer all to preserving pan; add water from pips. Put pips in muslin bag and suspend from handle of pan so bag rests in the water. Simmer 2–2½ hours, or until fruit is soft enough to disintegrate when pressed between finger and thumb. Remove bag of pips, pressing out all liquid against side of pan. Add heated sugar, stir until dissolved, then bring quickly to the boil. Keep at a steady, rolling boil for 10 minutes, then test for a set by putting a spoonful on a cold plate. It should form a soft jelly that wrinkles when pushed with the forefinger. Boil longer if necessary, but 20 minutes should be sufficient. Pot up into hot jars, cover with wax discs, cover when cold.

ORANGE JELLY MARMALADE

Preparation time   1–1½ hours, plus overnight soaking
Cooking time   2½–3 hours, plus overnight straining
To yield   4–5 lb.

You will need

1 lb. Seville oranges
1 lb. Jaffa oranges
3 lemons
4½ pints (U.S. 11¼ cups) water
granulated *or* lump sugar

Remove yellow part of peel from fruit, cut this into match like strips.
Tie them in a muslin bag, big enough to allow room to swell. Put in basin with 1 pint (U.S. 2½ cups) water. Cut up fruit coarsely without removing pips or pith; put in another bowl with remaining water. Leave overnight.
Next day, add bag of peel and water to fruit, put all in preserving pan and boil together steadily for 2–2½ hours.
Remove bag of peel and empty peel into a basin. Strain juice and pulp through jelly bag, leaving to drip overnight. Measure juice, put in pan.
Allow 1 lb. sugar to each pint (U.S. 2½ cups) juice. Heat slowly until sugar dissolves, then boil quickly for 20–25 minutes, or until a little tested on a cold plate sets in soft jelly. Add shredded peel, stir well, leave for a few minutes, then stir again and pot up.

FRUIT INTO JELLY

The process of jelly making is the same whatever fruit or mixture of fruits are used. Fruit is cooked in water to just cover it; the juice is strained overnight, then measured and sugar in the proportion of 1 lb. to each pint (U.S. 2½ cups) of juice is added and the two boiled until a good set is obtained.

The peel, cores, stalks and seeds of fruit contain pectin which is necessary to make the juice jell, so these should not be removed. Acid also is necessary to get a good set, so fruits that are deficient in acid are combined with acid fruits.
The cooked fruit is strained through a felt or flannel jelly bag which is suspended on a stand, or it can be hung on a hook with a basin underneath. Failing a jelly bag you can use a square of flannel or two or three thicknesses of muslin tied at each corner to the legs of an upturned stool, the basin standing on the upturned seat of the stool. Whatever straining bag you use it must be scalded first. Do not squeeze fruit.
Always *simmer* the fruit when cooking it to extract juice. *Never* allow the juice to boil until the sugar is dissolved.
The sugar being dissolved, boil *rapidly* until setting point is reached.
Skim only once, just before potting.
Jelly is best potted into small jars; flavour deteriorates if a large jar is opened and a quantity left unused for some time.
Do not expect your home-made fruit jelly to have the stiff texture of comercially fruit flavoured gelatine compounds.
Allow jellies to cool on a sunny window sill if possible; the sunshine improves the flavour.
Do not put lids on jars until jelly is quite cold.

A selection of preserves

TO TEST FOR A SET

Put a teaspoon of the jelly on a cold plate and leave for a few minutes in a cold place. Push the jelly with the side of your little finger; the jelly will wrinkle if it has reached setting point.

It is always difficult to estimate how much jelly you will get from a certain weight of fruit as it is impossible to know what juice yield there will be until the fruit is cooked, but 4–5 lb. of juicy fruit with 1 pint (U.S. 2½ cups) water should yield 1¾–2 pints (U.S. 4⅜–5 cups) jelly.

BLACKCURRANT JELLY

Preparation time 15–20 minutes
Cooking time 30 minutes, plus overnight straining
To yield 2 pints (U.S. 5 cups)

You will need

3 lb. blackcurrants
1½–2 pints (U.S. 3¾–5 cups) water
sugar

Wash currants; there is no need to remove stalks. Just cover with water and simmer until tender, mashing well. Strain and allow 1 lb. sugar to 1 pint (U.S. 2½ cups) juice. Proceed as for spiced apple jelly, see opposite.

GOOSEBERRY MINT JELLY

Preparation time 30 minutes
Cooking time 30 minutes
To yield ¾–1 pint (U.S. 1⅞–2½ cups)

You will need

2 lb. green gooseberries
¾ pint (U.S. 1⅞ cups) water
sugar
4 tablespoons vinegar
4 tablespoons chopped fresh mint

Wash gooseberries, split them and cook until reduced to a pulp. Strain through jelly bag. Measure liquid and allow 1 lb. sugar to each pint (U.S. 2½ cups). Put in pan with the vinegar and the mint. Boil steadily until a good set is reached, then strain into small pots and tie down at once.

Note

Most fruit jellies should be cold when tied down, but mint jelly is tied down hot as this prevents the mint rising.

SPICED APPLE JELLY

Preparation time 1 hour
Cooking time 1 hour 20 minutes, plus overnight straining
To yield 1¾–2 pints (U.S. 4⅜–5 cups)

You will need

4 lb. cooking apples
1–1½ pints (U.S. 2½–3¾ cups) water
3-inch stick cinnamon
6 cloves
sugar

Wash and weigh apples after removing bruised parts. Cut them up roughly, just cover with water, add spices, simmer 1 hour, stirring often. Strain through jelly bag or flannel, overnight. Measure juice: allow 1 lb. sugar to each pint (U.S. 2½ cups). Stir over a low heat until sugar dissolves; boil quickly until a good set is reached, see above for testing, about 15 minutes. Pour into heated jars; tie down when cold.

Marmalade making

Bottled whole tomatoes; pears preserved in syrup

PICKLES, CHUTNEYS AND VEGETABLE PRESERVATION

In one respect the modern British housewife is better off than her ancestors; she can buy excellent malt and wine vinegars and pickling spices without the trouble of blending and mixing her own. One modern refinement she must *not* use is refined table salt; the coarse, natural kind must be used.

The term 'mixed pickling spice' is rather vague; usually it consists of mustard seed, cloves, peppercorns, whole allspice, coriander, bay leaves, blade mace, root ginger; but really it is better to use the spices separately as tastes differ regarding pungency or mildness of pickles and chutneys. All vinegar must be boiled with the spices long enough to extract their flavour; a few of the spices can be added to the jars if you like a 'hot' pickle; two or three chillies in a jar of clear pickles look pretty through the glass. *Never* try to pickle anything in unboiled vinegar. It will soon go sour.

As almost every pickle or chutney recipe calls for spiced vinegar it is as well to have it at the start.

SPICED VINEGAR

Preparation time 10–15 minutes
Cooking time 4 minutes
To yield about 2 pints (U.S. 5 cups)

You will need

½ oz. peppercorns *
½ oz. allspice
¼ oz. blade mace
¼ oz. coriander seed
¼ oz. cloves
½ oz. bruised root ginger
3–4 chillies
¼ oz. mustard seed
6 dried bay leaves
¼ oz. coarse salt
2 pints (U.S. 5 cups) malt vinegar
* 2 oz. mixed pickling may be used in place of the various spices

Boil the spices and salt in the vinegar for 3–4 minutes. Strain and use. There will be a little evaporation. This is a mild pickle.

Most vegetables used in pickles have to be wet or dry salt brined before spiced vinegar is added to them; the salt acts as a preservative, helps to tenderise the vegetables and preserves colour.

STANDARD BRINE FOR PICKLES

8 oz. coarse salt to 3 pints (U.S. 7½ cups) water. Bring to boil and leave to go cold before using. Allow 1 pint (U.S. 2½ cups) brine to 1 lb. vegetables.

DRY BRINING

This is done by slicing or cutting up the vegetables and laying them on a shallow dish with a sprinkling of salt over the top if there is only one layer. This gives a strong brining, too salty for some people; the vegetables should be well drained of salt that has liquified in the dish.

PICKLES

PICCALILLI

Preparation time 40–50 minutes
Cooking time 25–30 minutes
To yield 5–6 lb.

You will need

3 lb. marrow, weight after preparing
1 lb. cauliflower
1 lb. shallots *or* pickling onions
8 oz. young dwarf beans *or* runner beans
8 oz. green tomatoes
coarse salt for dry brining, see page 115
4 pints (U.S. 10 cups) vinegar
$\frac{1}{4}$ oz. mustard seeds
6 crushed dried chillies
1 oz. cornflour
2 oz. powdered mustard
$\frac{1}{2}$ oz. turmeric
6 oz. granulated sugar

Peel marrow, remove seeds; cut into cubes or slices. Break cauliflower into small sprigs; the inner stalk of cauliflower pickles very well but discard hard bottom stump. Peel the shallots or onions; top and tail beans and slice if necessary. Cut the tomatoes into quarters, or eighths if large; mix vegetables, put on dish and dry brine them, see page 115. Leave overnight. Drain off liquid salt, put vegetables in pan. Cover with vinegar, reserving about $\frac{1}{2}$ pint (U.S. 1$\frac{1}{4}$ cups). Add mustard seeds and crushed chillies. Boil up; simmer 15 minutes. Mix the cornflour, mustard, turmeric and sugar, then blend to a smooth paste with remaining vinegar. Add this to the boiling pickle, stir well. Boil again, stirring all the time, 3–4 minutes. Pour off into hot jars; cover when cold. Ready after three days.

Note

There are many versions of piccalilli in Great Britain and in America; this is an old family recipe, semi sweet and aromatic and most people like it for its mildness. It must not be confused with mustard pickle which does not contain turmeric. Turmeric can be obtained from the chemists 'or herbalists'; few grocers stock it.

PICKLED EGGS

In the good old days when fresh eggs could be bought at less than a penny each it was the usual thing in country districts to pickle them either for use in salads or for first courses, or added to a casserole. In many bars in country pubs a jar of pickled eggs stands alongside the pickled onions to be eaten with a glass of beer or stout.

Preparation time 20–25 minutes
Cooking time 20 minutes
To yield 18 eggs

You will need

18 fresh eggs
2 pints (U.S. 5 cups) malt vinegar
1 oz. mixed pickling spice
$\frac{1}{2}$ oz. bruised root ginger
1 teaspoon coarse salt

Hard-boil eggs for 15 minutes, plunge into cold water and shell when cool enough to handle.
Pack them upright in wide mouthed glass jar.
Boil vinegar with spices and salt for 3 minutes and strain over the eggs.
Eggs should be completely covered. If liked, put a few spices on top of the jar and when cold cover the jar closely. The eggs will be ready for use after one month.

Pickled eggs

SWEET PICKLED ONIONS

Preparation time 1 hour
Cooking time 10–15 minutes, after soaking
To yield 3 1 lb. jars

You will need

2 lb. small onions *or* shallots
4 pints (U.S. 10 cups) water
¾ pint (U.S. 1⅞ cups) coarse salt
2 pints (U.S. 5 cups) spiced vinegar, see page 115
4 oz. Demerara sugar

Peel the onions or shallots, boil the water and salt, allow it to cool and pour over the onions. Leave for 2 days, then change the brine and leave for 2 days more. Put the onions into a pan with the spiced vinegar and the sugar and simmer for 10 minutes, put into jars and tie down when cold. Keep for 2–3 weeks before using.

PICKLED WALNUTS

Gather walnuts while young and green; they should be easily pierced with a fork. Prick them all over with fork, wear gloves to do this as they stain badly, put them in an old dish, cover with a strong brine, made with 1 lb. salt to 2 pints (U.S. 5 cups) water. Stand out of doors for 9 days turning them over in the brine every day, and changing the brine

Sweet pickled onions

every 3 days. Drain and spread on a tray in the sun until quite black. Put into jars and cover with cold spiced vinegar, see page 115. Do not tie down for a day or two, when walnuts will have soaked up some vinegar and will need to be covered with more. Ready in a month, but keep years.

PICKLED MUSHROOMS

Preparation time 5 minutes
Cooking time 10—15 minutes, see method
To yield 1 lb.

You will need

1 lb. button mushrooms
about 1 pint (U.S. 2½ cups) white vinegar
1 teaspoon salt
½ teaspoon white pepper
small piece root ginger
1 small onion, sliced

Clean mushrooms by wiping them over with a damp flannel dipped in salt; it is not necessary to peel them. Put into a pan with white vinegar to cover them, and add rest of ingredients. Simmer until mushrooms are tender, lift them out carefully and place in jar, then cover with hot vinegar. Cover and seal well.

PICKLED RED CABBAGE

Preparation time 30 minutes, plus overnight salting
Cooking time no cooking
To yield 3–4 1 lb. jars

You will need

1 firm red cabbage, 3–4 lb.
4 oz. coarse salt
3–4 pints (U.S. 7½–10 cups) spiced vinegar

Remove outer leaves from cabbage. Cut cabbage into quarters, remove hard centre stalk, shred cabbage finely. Separate shreds and dry brine them, see page 115. Leave overnight; drain off liquid salt, and pack the cabbage, not too tightly, into jars. Cover with cold spiced vinegar. Allow the vinegar to seep through cabbage, then top up with more vinegar before covering jars. Ready after a fortnight.

CLEAR MIXED PICKLES

Preparation time 1½ hours
Cooking time no cooking
To yield 3–4 1 lb. jars

You will need

1 firm cauliflower, about 1 lb.
8 oz. small pickling onions
8 oz. small ridge cucumbers
8 oz. green tomatoes
8 oz. dwarf beans
2–3 pints (U.S. 5–7½ cups) standard brine,
    see page 115
2–3 pints (U.S. 5–7½ cups) spiced vinegar,
    see page 115

Break cauliflower in small sprigs; skin onions, cut cucumbers, unpeeled, into cubes or 2–3-inch sticks, quarter tomatoes, top and tail beans and slice if large, but it is best to use small ones. Place all in bowl, cover with standard brine; leave for 24 hours. Drain, pack closely in jars. Cover with cold spiced vinegar, allowing it to seep through the vegetables; fill up with more vinegar if necessary before putting on lids. Leave to mature for at least a month.

PICKLED DAMSONS

Preparation time 45–50 minutes
Cooking time 25–30 minutes
To yield 6–7 1 lb. jars

You will need

6 lb. damsons
1½ pints (U.S. 3¾ cups) spiced vinegar,
    see page 115
3 lb. brown sugar

Stalk the damsons, wash them and prick all over with a fork.
Boil vinegar and brown sugar until syrupy, about 10–15 minutes, and add the damsons. Simmer until damsons are tender but not broken, about 10 minutes. Put them into jars, using perforated spoon. Boil vinegar up again, then pour it over the fruit. Cover immediately.

DAMSON CHEESE
OLD ENGLISH RECIPE

First stalk and wash as many damsons as you have, put them in a stone jar or casserole, cover and place in a slow oven (310°F. or Gas Mark 2) until juice runs, and stones are easily removed. Stir well; rub fruit through a sieve. Remove kernels from stones and add them to the pulp. Allow 1 lb. sugar to each lb. pulp. Heat sugar, mix with pulp and put in a pan. Boil until it jellies, then pour into small, straight sided jars. Put paper dipped in brandy on top of each and tie down at once. Best kept six months. The cheese will shrink a little from sides of jars and have a light crust of sugar.

Note

Instead of putting brandied paper on top, a bay leaf can be put on top of the cheese before tying the jars down.

PICKLED NASTURTIUM SEEDS
IMITATION CAPERS

Pick seeds on a dry day, before they have fallen. Dry them on a tray in the sun, or in a cool oven. Boil 1 pint (U.S. 2½ cups) vinegar with 2 bay leaves, 6 peppercorns and 1 teaspoon salt, remove from heat and leave to go cold. Pack seeds into dry bottles and cover with cold spiced vinegar, and cork bottles securely. Keep for several weeks before using.

RASPBERRY VINEGAR

Place 2 pints (U.S. 5 cups) fresh raspberries in a deep jar, pour over them 1 pint (U.S. 2½ cups) white vinegar, leave for 24 hours, then strain through muslin without pressing the fruit. Pour the liquid over another 2 pints (U.S. 5 cups) raspberries, and leave them for another 24 hours, strain again, and to every pint (U.S. 2½ cups) of liquid allow 1 lb. sugar.
Put into saucepan over low heat and stir until sugar dissolves, then boil for 10 minutes. Remove the scum, cool a little and pour into warm sterilised bottles. Cork well, and store in a cool place.

CHUTNEYS, KETCHUPS AND SAUCES

Chutneys are cooked mixed pickles in which fruits and vegetables are blended with spices and vinegar so that you get a sweet sour preserve. There is really no hard and fast rule either about the ingredients of chutney or about the quantity of spices and seasonings but apples appear in many of them as they form a pulp which gives 'body' to chutney.

You can make your chutney as sweet or hot as you like, according to your family's taste. Thus if you like a fairly mild chutney, decrease or leave out cayenne, ginger or chillies and use fewer peppercorns, and use more mustard seeds, mace, allspice, cinnamon, which are aromatic rather than hot.

Ketchup, catchup or catsup — Britain has never made up its mind — and sauces, are the extracted juices of vegetables or fruit preserved with spices, salt and vinegar.

APPLE CHUTNEY

Preparation time 1 hour
Cooking time 1 hour
To yield 6–7 1 lb. jars

You will need

4 lb. apples
2 lb. onions
8 oz. stoned raisins
8 oz. currants
1 lb. brown sugar
1–2 tablespoons treacle
1 tablespoon salt
pinch cayenne pepper
2 pints (U.S. 5 cups) spiced vinegar, see page 115

A selection of chutneys and preserves

Peel, core and chop the apples finely; peel and shred the onion, stone and chop raisins, clean the currants. Put all in pan with the remaining ingredients. Simmer gently 1 hour, stirring often. Put into jars with a few spices in each jar and tie down securely.

PLUM CHUTNEY

Preparation time 40–50 minutes
Cooking time 1½–1¾ hours
To yield 3–3½ lb.

You will need

2 lb. plums
1 lb. carrots
2 cloves garlic
1 pint (U.S. 2½ cups) vinegar
1 lb. Demerara sugar
¼ teaspoon cayenne pepper
2 oz. salt
½ oz. ground ginger
1 lb. dates, stoned and chopped

Stone and cut up plums; crack a few stones and take out the kernels.
Grate carrots and finely chop the garlic. Add the plums, kernels, carrots and garlic to the vinegar and boil steadily until soft, 45 minutes–1 hour.
Then add the sugar, cayenne pepper, salt, ground ginger and dates and boil for about 30 minutes, or until thick.

APPLE AND TOMATO CHUTNEY

Preparation time 30 minutes
Cooking time 2¼–2½ hours
To yield 3 lb.

You will need

1 lb. cooking apples
1 lb. onions
1 lb. ripe tomatoes
½ oz. mixed pickling spice
4 oz. sultanas
½ pint (U.S. 1¼ cups) vinegar
8 oz. black treacle
1 teaspoon salt
4 oz. mustard seeds *or* 1 oz. dry mustard

Peel and core the apples and chop into small cubes. Peel and chop onions. Skin tomatoes. Tie pickling spice in muslin. Place all ingredients in a pan and simmer for 2¼–2½ hours, until thick. Remove pickling spice and pot while still warm.

PEAR AND GINGER CHUTNEY

Preparation time 30 minutes
Cooking time 2 hours
To yield 3–3½ lb.

You will need

3 lb. pears
1 lb. onions
1 orange
1 lemon
8 oz. granulated sugar
8 oz. raisins
½ pint (U.S. 1¼ cups) spiced vinegar, see page 115
½ level teaspoon powdered clove
1 level teaspoon ground ginger
1 level teaspoon salt
few drops chilli sauce

Peel, core and chop the pears. Chop the onions. Grate the rind of the orange and lemon and squeeze out the juice. Add to all the remaining ingredients in a large saucepan. Bring to the boil and simmer for 2 hours. Pot up in hot jars and seal.

Apple and tomato chutney

MUSHROOM KETCHUP

Preparation time 30 minutes
Cooking time 1½ hours, after brining
To yield ¾–1 pint (U.S. 1⅞–2½ cups)

You will need

4 lb. black mushrooms
3 oz. coarse salt
½ pint (U.S. 1¼ cups) vinegar
1 onion
1 clove garlic
1 teaspoon mixed pickling spice
¼ teaspoon grated nutmeg

Stalk and skin the mushrooms, sprinkle under sides with salt and leave for an hour or so, then wipe with a towel; wash stalks. Place mushrooms with stalks in a bowl, sprinkle salt over them, stand in a cool place, and leave for 3 days, stirring daily with wooden spoon.
Then add all the other ingredients, and simmer for 1 hour.
Strain into sterilised bottles with screw tops. Fasten corks loosely and stand bottles in a pan of water reaching to necks of bottles. Bring slowly to boiling point and keep at this temperature for 20 minutes. Then take up and cork with sterilised corks, and put on screw caps tightly.
Mushroom ketchup can be used as a condiment or to flavour soup or stews.

TOMATO SAUCE
(FOR KEEPING)

Preparation time 20–25 minutes
Cooking time 1 hour 10 minutes
To yield 1 pint (U.S. 2½ cups)

You will need

3 lb. ripe tomatoes
4 oz. onions
1 pint (U.S. 2½ cups) spiced vinegar, see page 115
pinch cayenne pepper
4 tablespoons dry mustard
1 dessertspoon cornflour

Cut tomatoes and onions into small pieces. Put into pan with rest of ingredients except cornflour. Bring to the boil and simmer 1 hour. Cool and rub through a sieve. Return to pan, adding the cornflour blended with a little vinegar. Simmer and stir until the consistency of thick cream. Bottle in sterilised bottles with screw caps and coat caps with melted wax.

MINT SAUCE
(FOR KEEPING)

Preparation time 20–25 minutes
Cooking time 5–10 minutes
To yield 1½ pints (U.S. 3¾ cups)

You will need

8 oz. mint leaves
1 pint (U.S. 2½ cups) vinegar
12 oz. sugar
pinch powdered borax

Wash, dry and chop finely the freshly gathered mint. Boil the vinegar with the sugar and borax until sugar dissolves.
Half fill bottles with mint. Fill up with cooled vinegar. The bottles should have screw tops or very tight fitting corks.
Dip the necks of the bottles in melted paraffin wax to be sure they are airtight.

BROWN SPICE SAUCE
(STEAK SAUCE)

Preparation time 30 minutes
Cooking time 25–30 minutes
To yield 1–1½ pints (U.S. 2½–3¾ cups)

You will need

1 lb. shallots, chopped
1 teaspoon black pepper
1 tablespoon black treacle
1 teaspoon salt
1 clove garlic, crushed
¼ oz. chillies
1 tablespoon mushroom ketchup
1 tablespoon anchovy paste
¼ oz. ground cloves
1 pint (U.S. 2½ cups) malt vinegar

Put all ingredients into a pan, except vinegar, and just cover with cold water, boil up, and simmer until shallots are reduced to a pulp. Strain through a sieve, pressing well, then return to pan with vinegar, boil up for 2–3 minutes and bottle. If a thicker sauce is liked, add 1 dessertspoon cornflour mixed to a smooth paste with a little vinegar. This is not a long keeping sauce, but will certainly last a few weeks.

ROSE HIP SYRUP

Pick only fully ripe, red berries, and use them when fresh.
Allow 3 pints (U.S. 7½ cups) boiling water to 2 lb. hips. Crush them and put into the boiling water, boil up, stir well, then stand aside for 15 minutes. Strain through flannel jelly bag without pressing, and when all dripping has ceased, return pulp to the pan with another pint (U.S. 2½ cups) water. Boil again and leave for another 15 minutes. Strain and mix the two liquids together. Boil until reduced to 1½ pints (U.S. 3¾ cups). Add 1 lb. sugar, stir until dissolved, boil up and cool slightly. Fill sterilised bottles to within 1½-inches of the top, cork loosely with sterilised corks, stand in pan of water reaching almost to tops of bottles, bring to simmering point and hold at this temperature for 10 minutes. Remove bottles, wire on the corks or cover with screw caps.

PRESERVING BY DRYING AND SALTING

SALTING BEANS

(Illustrated in colour on opposite page)

Surplus dwarf or runner beans can be preserved by packing them in salt in glass or unglazed earthenware jar. The jar should be wide necked so that you can easily get your hand inside it to press down the beans. It is not necessary to completely fill the jar all at one go; in a garden beans come to perfection day by day, more than one wants for the day's meal. When this happens the surplus can be added to the jar. Coarse cooking salt should be used. Crystallised sea salt is the 'saltiest' for this purpose. Allow 1 lb. salt to every 3 lb. beans. Wash, top and tail beans and remove strings if necessary. Small beans can be salted whole or snapped into pieces. Runner beans should be sliced. Put a good layer of salt in the jar, then a layer of beans about 1-inch in depth and continue with the alternate layers until jar is full, pressing each layer of beans well down. Finish with a layer of salt.

Cover the jar loosely and let it stand for a few days. The beans will settle in the jar, leaving room for another layer of beans and salt but finish off with salt. Cover jar closely with waxed paper, no metal must come in contact with salt. Store in a cool, dry, dark place. It helps to keep the beans a good colour by keeping them in the dark, but there will be a slight darkening of the beans in time.

To cook salted beans, take out as many as required, wash well in cold water and leave in cold water for about 2 hours. Then rinse them again and cook in unsalted water until tender.

DRIED MUSHROOMS

(Illustrated in colour on opposite page)

The best mushrooms for drying are the field variety. These are not so easy to come by these days as so many fields have been ploughed up and the use of artificial manures in place of farm manure has meant the disappearance of wild mushrooms.

On misty autumn mornings they do appear in some districts and it is sometimes possible to buy them in some town greengrocers very cheaply when there is a sudden glut.

It is worth while drying mushrooms as they are so useful for making soups and flavouring stews, and after soaking they can be fried or grilled. Mushrooms for drying must be fresh and well open; the button or half closed kind are not really suitable. Remove stems, these can be used in soup or stews, peel mushrooms if they are very dirty, but when fresh just wipe with a damp cloth. Then thread them on fine string with a knot between each to prevent touching and hang to dry in a warm airy place.

The edge of a kitchen shelf is quite good so long as no steam can get to them.

Alternatively, suspend them on a rack in a very cool oven (150°F. or less than Gas Mark ¼) with a solid fuel range they can be placed over the range. The mushrooms will become the texture of chamois leather.

Store in a jar in a dry place or they can hang in the kitchen so long as they are free from dust and steam.

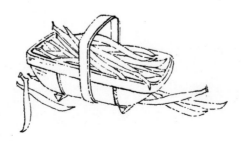

Salting beans and dried mushrooms

Assorted loaves and buns

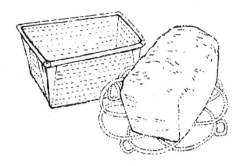

BREADS, BUNS AND SCONES

In old British cookery, baking day was literally a day dedicated to baking. The brick oven had to be specially heated inside with 'faggots' or bundles of brushwood, and on top of them larger wood to make a solid fire. As the wood burnt up, more was added, and finally two or three large logs were thrown in, the door securely closed and the logs left to burn until reduced to glowing red ashes. Then the oven was opened and the ashes spread from middle to sides so the whole floor was heated evenly. As the ashes cooled they were scraped out and fell through a slot in front of the oven door into the ash-hole. A large mop was soaked in hot water and rubbed over every part of the oven and the door closed leaving a little steam inside.

This operation alone would take anything from one to two hours, so it is not surprising that having got the oven hot the fullest use was made of it, baking the week's batch of bread, tarts and pies, and as the heat gradually lowered, gingerbread and oatcakes, fruit cakes and biscuits, and in the last heat drying breadcrumbs and herbs.

The coming of the coal fired kitchen range with side oven did not see much change in the baking day habit, for though the oven was not heated from within with wood, a good fire had to be stoked up and flues nicely adjusted to get the heat going where you wanted it, which was under the oven and round over the top of it. And if the wind happened to be in the wrong direction, the flues unswept or the coal of poor quality it sometimes took as long for the oven to get hot as did the old

brick oven, so it was as well to have a 'real good do' while you were about the baking.

People who remember bread baked in the old brick oven and side oven say that no bread baked in modern ovens tastes the same; there was a nutty 'oven' taste that you don't get with gas or electric cookers. I am inclined to agree with them, having baked bread in the old kitchen oven. All the same, home-made bread from any oven is superior in taste and goodness to bakery bread. We can now be sure of getting our ovens to the right temperature with gas and electric cookers and the modern solid fuel range gives even better results than its dirty and tiresome ancestor. A once a week baking of bread will serve the average family as the bread keeps fresh for a week.

While the dough is rising you can do other jobs; once it is in the oven it 'looks after itself' and you can cook other things while the oven is hot.

Today it is not always easy to buy fresh yeast; I believe in the North, grocer still sell it, but in the South I always have to go to my friendly baker. Fresh yeast is the best but you can get good results from dried yeast. It is a little more trouble as it must be reconstituted before use. You need less weight of dry yeast than the fresh, since the moisture has been taken from it, usually half as much dry yeast as the fresh, but when the water is put back the weight is the same. It is not necessary to cream fresh yeast with the sugar when making plain bread; this wastes time and results are just as good if the yeast is crumbled into a well in the flour and the sugar and warm liquid added.

PLAIN BREAD DOUGH

The quantities given are sufficient to make four small tin loaves, or two cottage loaves, or two plaits, or two tin loaves and one round Coburg type loaf, or two small loaves and twelve breakfast rolls, or twenty four breakfast rolls.

Preparation time 1½ hours, including sponging, kneading, rising
Cooking time 45 minutes
To make 4 small loaves

You will need

3 lb. plain flour
2 level teaspoons salt
1 oz. fresh yeast *or* ½ oz. dried yeast
1 rounded teaspoon sugar
2 oz. lard
about 1½ pints (U.S. 3¾ cups) lukewarm water

Sift warmed flour and salt into warmed mixing bowl reserving about two tablespoons to help in mixing the dough.

Make a well in the middle of flour and crumble fresh yeast into it and sprinkle with sugar. Pour in half the lukewarm water and sprinkle a little flour on top of water. Leave in warm place until yeast rises on top of water, about 10–15 minutes. If dried yeast is used, put it into a jug with the sugar and half the water, sprinkle tablespoon of flour on top and leave in warm place until yeast rises to top of water, about 10 minutes, then pour into the well in centre of flour. When yeast has risen, add lard, cut into small pieces, to yeast and water mixture. Pour in most of the remaining lukewarm water and stir in flour with a knife. When all the flour is stirred in, making a rather ropy mixture, start kneading with the floured hands, adding more water gradually if dough becomes too stiff to knead, but take care not to get it too soft. Keep the sides of the bowl and your hands sprinkled with the reserved two tablespoons of flour, to prevent sticking.

When all flour is mixed in, making a smooth elastic dough, continue kneading with firm steady punches with the fist for a further 10 minutes or so; pull dough from sides to middle, pressing it well down with a firm rhythmic movement. When dough is smooth and elastic and no longer sticks to the side of the bowl or your hands, form it into a round and turn it over in the floured bowl so that the smooth, round side is on top, make two slashes across the top and cover with a warm, damp tea towel. Stand the bowl in a warm place, away from draughts, until dough has risen to double its first size. This will take about 1 hour.

TO MAKE LOAVES

(Illustrated in colour on page 124)

Pre-heat oven to very hot (450°F. or Gas Mark 8), with shelf on middle runner.
Brush oblong loaf tins with melted fat. Turn the risen dough out onto floured board and knock it back with the knuckles quickly. This distributes the gas bubbles and evens out the texture. Divide dough into four. Knead and roll each piece into a sausage shape the length of the tin. Place smooth side up in the tin, prick top or make two or three short cuts across top, and leave in a warm place, covered, to rise twice its first size. Then bake the loaves on middle shelf of oven for 30–35 minutes, until a rich brown and slightly shrunk from sides of tins and sound hollow when knocked with the knuckles. Half way through the baking twist the loaves around so that they brown evenly. Remove loaves from tins immediately they are baked and leave to cool standing on one end.

TO MAKE PLAITS

(Illustrated in colour on page 124)

Cut risen and 'knocked back' dough in halves. Cut each half into three equal pieces and roll each in floured hands into a long sausage shape about 12-inches long. Pinch three ends together and put a weight on the end to keep the dough steady while you plait the strands loosely. Pinch the ends firmly together and with the sides of your hands gently press both ends so that the plait is narrower at the ends than the middle. Place the plaits on a greased baking sheet and leave to rise 15–20 minutes. Brush over with beaten egg or milk and bake in very hot oven 20–25 minutes.

TO MAKE COTTAGE LOAVES

(Illustrated in colour on page 124)

Cut risen and 'knocked back' dough into thirds. Cut one third in half again so you have two large pieces and two small pieces. Knead larger pieces into rounds, then flatten them slightly with the palm of your hand. Knead smaller pieces into rounds and flatten slightly. Dampen larger pieces with a little beaten egg or milk and press smaller pieces onto dampened portion, pressing them firmly down. Then flour two first fingers of one hand and push them right through centre of the loaf. Place on greased baking sheet and leave to rise about 30 minutes, or until double the first size. Then bake in centre of very hot oven, 35–40 minutes, or until a good brown and hollow sounding when rapped with the knuckles.

TO MAKE BREAD ROLLS

(Illustrated in colour on page 124)

For 12 rolls, divide given quantity of dough in half and cut one half into 12 equal portions. Knead each on floured board into smooth rounds or sausage shapes. Place well apart on greased baking sheet. Leave to rise about 15 minutes or until double their first size. Brush tops with warm milk and bake in very hot oven 12–15 minutes. Cool, uncovered, on wire tray.

TO MAKE COBURG LOAF

Cut the risen and 'knocked back' dough in halves. Knead one half firmly on floured board, working into a ball. Place on a greased baking sheet and press lightly with flat of your hand. Leave to rise for 15 minutes then make a shallow cross with a knife on top of loaf. Bake in middle of very hot oven 30–35 minutes. Brush over with warm milk and return to oven for a few minutes to dry and crisp; cool on wire tray.

LARDY CAKE

Preparation time 25–30 minutes
Cooking time 1½ hours, including rising

You will need

1 lb. plain bread dough which has risen once, see page 126
6 oz. lard
6 oz. granulated sugar
4 oz. currants
½ teaspoon mixed spice
little sugar and water glaze, see page 130

Roll out dough to an oblong on floured board and put on half the lard in dabs to cover two thirds of length surface, as in making flaky pastry. Sprinkle well with the sugar, fruit and spice. Fold dough into three, folding the unlarded piece over first. Turn to the right, seal open ends, and repeat sugaring, larding and folding. Turn to the right again and roll once more. Fold again and this time roll to fit a Yorkshire pudding tin, 12-inches by 7-inches. Put to rise in warm place, covered with

Lardy cake

tea towel, to rise to half its height, about ¾ hour. Cook in middle of oven (400°F. or Gas Mark 6), for about 45 minutes. Half way through cooking, brush over with a thick sugar glaze. Serve hot.

YORKSHIRE SCONES

(Illustrated in colour on page 133)

Preparation time 15 minutes
Cooking time 15–20 minutes
To make 8

You will need

8 oz. flour
¼ teaspoon bicarbonate of soda
½ teaspoon cream of tartar
¼ teaspoon salt
3 oz. sugar
3 oz. butter *or* lard
2 oz. sultanas
½ oz. chopped candied peel
1 egg
little milk

Sieve all dry ingredients together, rub in the fat, add the sultanas and peel, and stir in the beaten egg and mix to stiff dough with milk. Divide in two, roll into rounds on floured board, place on baking sheet and mark each round into triangles. Bake in a moderately hot oven (375°F. or Gas Mark 5), for 15–20 minutes.

BROWN BREAD

Preparation time 30–35 minutes
Cooking time 1½ hours
To make 2 loaves

You will need

12 oz. wholemeal flour
12 oz. plain flour
1 rounded dessertspoon sugar
1½ level teaspoons salt
1 oz. fresh yeast *or* ½ oz. dried yeast
1 oz. table margarine, melted
¾ pint (U.S. 1⅞ cups) lukewarm water

Put flours, sugar and salt into a warmed mixing bowl, crumble the fresh yeast and rub it into the dry mixture. Add the melted margarine and mix to a soft dough with the water, using a wooden spoon and then kneading with the hand.
If dried yeast is used, sprinkle the yeast and sugar on top of ½ pint (U.S. 1¼ cups) of the lukewarm water and leave in a warm place for about 10 minutes or until frothy. Put flour and salt into mixing bowl. Add yeast mixture, melted margarine and remaining ¼ pint (U.S. ⅝ cup) water and finish kneading as with fresh yeast.
Divide dough into two equal portions and mould them into smooth sausage shapes large enough to half fill two greased 1 lb. tins. Place dough smooth side up in the tins, cover with a warm, damp tea towel and leave to rise in a warm place for 30–40 minutes, or until dough reaches tops of tins. Bake in a very hot oven (450°F. or Gas Mark 8) for 40–50 minutes. Loaves should sound hollow when rapped with knuckles. Cool on a wire tray.

TO MAKE FLOWER POT LOAF

(Illustrated in colour on page 124)

Use a new or well scrubbed flower pot. Brush the inside well with melted lard and bake it for an hour or so in a moderate oven to season it. After this treatment the flower pot will not need seasoning again. Keep the pot especially for baking. Put a piece of foil over hole in bottom of pot.
Roll half the dough into a short fat roll. Grease the flower pot again after seasoning it, and put the roll of dough inside. Press it lightly until it fits smoothly into the pot, then leave to rise until dough reaches to top of pot. Bake in very hot oven (450°F. or Gas Mark 8), for 35 minutes then reduce heat to moderate (350°F. or Gas Mark 4) for a further 10 minutes. Cool on wire tray.

Scotch pancakes

SCOTCH PANCAKES

(Illustrated in colour on page 143)

Preparation time 10 minutes
Cooking time 15–20 minutes
To make 12–14

You will need

8 oz. plain flour
½ teaspoon bicarbonate of soda
½ teaspoon cream of tartar
¼ teaspoon salt
1 oz. castor sugar
2 small eggs
½ pint (U.S. 1¼ cups) sour milk

Sieve all dry ingredients into mixing bowl; stir in beaten eggs, add half the milk and beat well for at least a minute. Add more milk to make the consistency of thick cream; stir well but do not beat. Grease a girdle or thick frying pan with a film of olive oil or unsalted butter; when hot drop the batter in tablespoonfuls onto it, making rounds about 4-inches across, and 3–4-inches apart. Cook until bubbles appear on top of pancakes and mixture sets, then turn with a palette knife and cook until golden brown on second side, 4–5 minutes in all. Grease girdle or pan afresh for each batch of pancakes. Cool on a tea towel and serve cold with butter and jam.

OATIES (SCOTTISH)

Preparation time 20 minutes
Cooking time 20 minutes
To make 8–10

You will need

4 oz. plain flour
2 level teaspoons baking powder
½ level teaspoon salt
4 oz. rolled oats
2 oz. castor sugar
3 oz. black treacle
4 oz. butter or margarine
coarse oatmeal, to sprinkle

Sieve flour, baking powder and salt together, add oats. Put sugar, black treacle and butter or margarine into a saucepan and heat until just melted. Mix this into the flour, etc. and stir until all ingredients are thoroughly combined.

Press into a greased 7-inch sandwich tin and bake in the centre of a moderate oven (350°F. or Gas Mark 4), for 20 minutes. Sprinkle the surface of the oaties with coarse oatmeal. Cut into wedges before the mixture cools.

BANNOCKS

Preparation time 1 hour 40 minutes
Cooking time 20 minutes
To make 8 bannocks

You will need

BATTER INGREDIENTS

2 oz. strong plain flour
1 oz. melted butter *or* lard
⅛ pint (U.S. scant ⅜ cup) warm milk
¼ oz. fresh yeast *or* ½ teaspoon dried yeast, reconstituted

ADDITIONAL INGREDIENTS

6 oz. strong plain flour
1 oz. castor sugar
⅛ pint (U.S. scant ⅜ cup) warm milk
1 oz. sultanas
1 oz. currants
½ oz. candied peel
milk for brushing

Bannocks

Blend batter ingredients together in a mixing bowl and leave for 20–30 minutes until batter is frothy. Add additional ingredients and mix well. Knead dough thoroughly for about 10 minutes on a lightly floured board.

Put dough to rise until it springs back when pressed gently with a floured finger, about 1 hour.

Knead dough once again and then shape into a ball. Flatten with the hands or rolling pin to approximately 8-inches across and ½-inch thick.

Put on a greased and floured tray and slash with sharp knife into 8 equal sections. Brush top with milk. Cover and rise again until dough feels springy, about 30 minutes. Brush top once again with a little milk.

Bake towards top of a moderately hot oven (400°F. or Gas Mark 6) for 15–20 minutes.

Cool on a wire tray.

Note

Traditionally, the bannock was made from oats and barley. It was moulded into a flat round cake, marked into 8 segments and then baked on an iron griddle over an open fire of wood or peat. Scots have long memories, bannocks are made in memory of the Battle of Bannockburn fought 650 years ago!

Our bannock is made from a rich yeast dough with the extra goodness of butter, milk and fruit, but we keep the traditional shape and marking.

FRUIT LOAF

(Illustrated in colour on page 124)

Preparation time 1 hour including rising
Cooking time 1¼ hours
To make 1 large loaf

You will need

10 oz. plain flour
½ teaspoon salt
½ oz. fresh yeast *or* ¼ oz. dried yeast
1 oz. castor sugar
2 oz. table margarine
1 small egg, beaten
6 oz. cleaned currants
¼ pint (U.S. ⅝ cups) lukewarm milk
egg *or* milk, to brush

Sift flour and salt into warmed bowl, reserving 1 tablespoonful, make a well in centre and crumble the fresh yeast into it. Sprinkle the sugar over yeast, and pour milk over it. Add a little flour from sides of bowl and stir it lightly into the milk and yeast mixture. Leave in a warm place until yeast froths up to top of liquid. Then add the melted margarine, the egg and milk and scatter the currants over the flour. Mix to a smooth dough, using a knife till flour is mixed in, then knead with the hand until a smooth elastic dough is formed. Sprinkle sides of bowl with flour once or twice to prevent sticking. Turn dough out onto a floured board and give it a quite light kneading for 2 or 3 minutes, return it to the bowl, cover with a damp tea towel and leave to rise in a warm place for about 40 minutes or until twice its size. Turn out dough onto a floured board and knock it back to press out air bubbles. Then knead and roll into a fat sausage shape and place in a well greased 2 lb. loaf tin. Leave to rise for 30 minutes or until double its size. Brush with egg or milk, then bake in hot oven (425°F. or Gas Mark 7) on middle shelf for 20 minutes, then in a moderately hot oven (350°F. or Gas Mark 5) for a further 25–30 minutes. Turn out of tin and glaze immediately.

TO MAKE THE GLAZE

Place 2 rounded tablespoons sugar and 3 tablespoons water in small saucepan over low heat; stir until dissolved, then boil rapidly, without stirring, 1–2 minutes. Cool slightly before using.

Muffins

MUFFINS

Preparation time 1¾ hours
Cooking time 10 minutes for each muffin
To make 6–8

You will need

1 lb. plain flour
1 teaspoon salt
2 teaspoons sugar
¾ oz. yeast
scant ½ pint (U.S. 1¼ cups) warm milk
1 egg, beaten
1 oz. butter, melted

Sieve flour and salt. Put sugar and crumbled yeast in well in centre of flour, add about a third of the milk over the yeast and leave to stand for 10 minutes. Mix beaten egg and melted butter and half remaining milk. When yeast has risen to top of liquid in flour bowl mix and knead with the egg and butter liquid, adding remaining milk gradually until a fairly soft dough is formed. Use as little flour as possible in the mixing. Leave the dough to rise in a warm place 50 minutes to 1 hour, then knock it back and re-roll it on a floured board to ½-inch thickness. Cut out with a pastry cutter into 3–3½-inch rounds. Place on a well floured board and dust tops liberally with flour. Leave to rise for 30 minutes in a warm place. Lightly grease a hot griddle or thick frying pan, transfer the muffins carefully from the board to the pan, and bake them two or three at a time 5 minutes each side, until golden brown. Turn them 2 or 3 times to make sure they are baked through.

Date and walnut tea bread

DATE AND WALNUT TEA BREAD

Preparation time 5–8 minutes
Cooking time 1–1¼ hours
To make 1 2 lb. loaf

You will need

12 oz. self-raising flour
¼ level teaspoon mixed spice
4 oz. luxury margarine
2 oz. castor sugar
1 egg
¼ pint (U.S. ⅝ cup) milk
2 oz. walnuts, chopped
2 oz. dates, chopped
3 level teaspoons black treacle

Sieve flour and spice, add remaning ingredients and mix together thoroughly with a wooden spoon for 2–3 minutes.
Place the mixture in a 2 lb. loaf tin, previously bottom lined with greaseproof paper and brushed on the inside with melted margarine.
Bake on middle shelf of a moderate oven (360°F. or Gas Mark 4), for 1 hour–1¼ hours. When cooked leave in the tin for 2–3 minutes, then turn out and cool on wire tray.
Decorate with glacé cherries and angelica leaves; sprinkle with icing sugar. Slice and spread with butter.

PIKELETS OR CRUMPETS

Cream ¼ oz. yeast and 1 teaspoon sugar with a little of the 1 pint (U.S. 2½ cups) tepid milk and water, add the rest, and pour into the sieved 1 lb. flour and 1 teaspoon salt. Mix and beat thoroughly for 5–10 minutes, stand in a warm place, covered, to rise, for 1 hour. Dissolve ¼ teaspoon bicarbonate of soda in a teaspoon warm water and add to the risen mixture and put to rise again for another 30 minutes. Have a hot greased girdle, or electric hot plate, or thick frying pan; place greased rings or large pastry cutters on greased surface, and drop spoonfuls of the mixture inside the rings to three-quarters fill them. Allow to cook until top is set and full of holes, and underside a biscuit colour. Remove the rings, turn the pikelets and allow to dry for a few minutes on underside. Leave to go cold. Serve toasted on both sides.

HOT CROSS BUNS

Follow the recipe for tea cakes, see page 132, but add 1 level teaspoon mixed cake spice and form the dough into small buns. Mark a cross with the back of a knife, strip of pastry or strips of candied peel. Glaze the buns with a little sugar and water glaze, see page 130, as soon as they are removed from the oven.

Hot cross buns

YORKSHIRE TEA CAKES

(Illustrated in colour on opposite page)

Preparation time 1 hour 40 minutes
Cooking time 25–30 minutes
To yield 8–10 teacakes

You will need

2 lb. plain flour
½ teaspoon salt
2 oz. lard *or* butter
2 oz. cleaned currants
1½ oz. yeast
1 teaspoon sugar
½ pint (U.S. 1¼ cups) milk
¼ pint (U.S. ⅝ cup) hot water
1 egg

Warm an earthenware bowl, warm flour, reserve
a little for mixing. Sieve flour and salt into the bowl,
rub in the lard or butter, add currants and make
a well in the middle. Cream the yeast with a
teaspoon sugar, mix the milk and water. Add half
the milk and water to the creamed yeast and sugar
and leave for 15 minutes, or until bubbles appear
on top. Mix to a dough with beaten egg and
remaining liquid, adding a sprinkling of flour
when necessary, and kneading till dough is
smooth and leaves sides of bowl clean. Form into
a round, turn dough over, make one or two slashes
on top, cover with a warm cloth and leave to rise
until double original size, about 1 hour. Divide
into 8–10 pieces, shape into round cakes about
1-inch thick, place on greased baking sheet well
apart and leave to rise for a further 15 minutes.
Bake in a hot oven (425°F. or Gas Mark 7) for
25–30 minutes, but do not let them get too brown.
Leave to cool, tilted against wall or shelf.

CHELSEA BUNS

(Illustrated in colour on page 124)

Preparation time 1½–1¾ hours
Cooking time 25 minutes
To make 10–12 buns

You will need

1 lb. plain flour
1½ teaspoons salt
1 oz. lard
½ oz. yeast
1 teaspoon castor sugar
½ pint (U.S. 1¼ cups) warm milk
2 oz. sugar
2 oz. currants

FOR THE GLAZE

1 tablespoon granulated sugar
2 tablespoons water

Sieve warmed flour and salt and rub in lard. Cream
yeast with castor sugar and add warm milk. Make
a well in flour and add liquid. Knead well, cover
with cloth and leave to rise in a warm place until
dough is double in size. Knead dough on floured
board lightly until smooth and roll out to an
oblong. Sprinkle with sugar and currants and roll
up like a Swiss roll. Cut into slices about 1-inch
thick and place in a greased straight sided baking
tin, close together so that the buns will join together
while cooking. Leave to prove for about 20 minutes
and bake in a hot oven (450 °F. or Gas Mark 8), for
about 15–20 minutes, until the buns are golden.
Just before the buns are completely cooked, brush
over with a sugar glaze made by boiling granulated
sugar in the water.

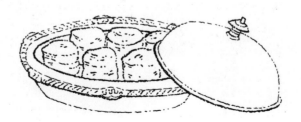

Yorkshire tea cakes; Yorkshire scones

Christmas fare

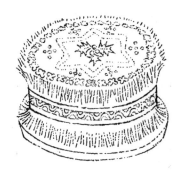

CAKES

Any foreigner reading about British food customs and traditions might think that every occasion, large or small was (and still is) an excuse for making a cake. He would be right; celebration cakes have always been a peculiar part of traditional British cooking — not so important now perhaps, when domestic cake-making is apt to depend on the contents of a packet rather than the skill of the cook. The days when the measure of a good cook was her success in making a good sponge or rich fruit cake are no more. But public events, anniversaries, sporting triumphs and such-like are still marked by the making of monumental, lavishly decorated cakes, grotesque or beautiful, and quite often inedible.

The enthusiasm for cake-making in the old days no doubt grew because tea was a 'proper' meal, and a cake for tea was a must.

Also the kitchen range was always at the ready and it seemed a natural thing to fill it with cakes or buns after the main cooking.

It seems that practically every town or county in Britain has its cake or bun, though in some cases there is little difference between them. Scotland is known as the 'Land o' Cakes' but cakes are no more prolific there than in the rest of Britain, except perhaps for scones and pancakes — though Wales would challenge her in this.

At one time it was the custom to have some kind of hot cakes for tea. These were always small buns, scones or pancakes and were often baked on a griddle or girdle over the open fire; or simply mixed scones or buns baked just before tea-time. As all these last-minute teatime cakes contain a small proportion of fat and eggs (depending on baking powder or cream of tartar for rising) they do not keep well from day to day, and never seem quite the same when reheated.

MINCE PIES

(Illustrated in colour on opposite page)

Preparation time 40–45 minutes, after mincemeat is made
Cooking time 15–20 minutes
To make 12 pies

You will need

8 oz. flan pastry, see page 78
1 lb. mincemeat

Roll out pastry thinly and cut into 24 rounds using a cutter a little larger than the patty tin to be used. Line tins with half the rounds and place a heaped teaspoon of mincemeat in each. Brush round edges of the remaining rounds with water. Place over the filled rounds, pressing edges well together. Make a hole in the centre of each with a skewer. Bake in hot oven (400°F. or Gas Mark 6), for about 20 minutes until pastry is a good golden brown. Sprinkle with castor sugar just before serving.

very moderate (335°F. or Gas Mark 3) and bake for 2–2¼ hours longer. Cover top with paper if it gets too brown.

Note

Brandy may be omitted and same quantity of lemon juice used.

RICH DUNDEE CAKE (SCOTTISH)

Preparation time 25–30 minutes
Cooking time 2¾–3 hours

You will need

7 oz. butter
7 oz. castor sugar
4 eggs
1 tablespoon brandy
8 oz. self-raising flour
¼ teaspoon salt
1 level teaspoon mixed cake spice
grated rind 1 lemon
14 oz. mixed dried fruit, including candied peel
1 oz. blanched almonds, chopped
2 oz. whole almonds, blanched

Line a 7–8-inch cake tin with two layers of grease-proof paper; grease side of paper that will be next to the cake. Cream butter and sugar, add well beaten eggs one at a time, adding a little flour between each egg to prevent curdling; add the brandy. Sift flour, salt and spice; add grated lemon rind, stir into the creamed mixture. Add cleaned fruit and chopped almonds, and if necessary, a little milk to make a stiffly dropping consistency, but do not make it too moist. Mix thoroughly; put into prepared tin. Make a slight depression in centre. Arrange the whole blanched almonds on top. Bake in a moderate oven (350°F. or Gas Mark 4), for the first 45 minutes, then reduce heat to

ENGLISH CHRISTMAS CAKE

(Illustrated in colour on page 134)

Preparation time 1–1½ hours
Cooking time 3–3½ hours

You will need

10 oz. self-raising flour
½ teaspoon salt
1 level teaspoon mixed cake spice
1 small nutmeg, grated
12 oz. currants
12 oz. sultanas
4 oz. chopped candied peel
2 oz. glacé cherries, quartered
2 oz. blanched almonds, chopped
grated rind 1 lemon and 1 orange
8 oz. butter
8 oz. soft brown sugar
4 large eggs
1 tablespoon dark treacle
1 tablespoon brandy *or* rum

Line an 8-inch round cake tin with two layers of greaseproof paper. Grease tin first and grease side of the paper that will be next to the cake. Allow paper lining side of tin to come 2-inches above rim. Sieve flour, salt and spices together into a bowl; rub currants and raisins in tea towel. Add chopped peel and glacé cherries, chopped almonds, lemon and orange rind to fruit. Mix well. Cream butter and sugar in large mixing bowl; add eggs one at a time, beat well and add a tablespoon of flour mixture between each egg to prevent curdling. Beat well after last egg is added, then add remaining flour and fruit in alternate spoonfuls to creamed mixture. After all fruit is added, stir in treacle, mixing it thoroughly, and lastly add the brandy. The mixture should be quite stiff but not crumbly; if it seems a little too stiff, add a little lemon or orange juice.

Put mixture into prepared tin, spoonful by spoonful, pressing it down so there are no air pockets. Smooth top with a knife dipped in hot water, leaving a slight hollow in the middle so that the cake will rise level; stand cake tin on a thick baking sheet and place in the middle of the pre-heated oven (310°F. or Gas Mark 2), and bake for 1 hour, then reduce heat to (290°F. or Gas Mark 1), and bake for a further 2½ hours. Half way through baking place a sheet of paper across top of cake so that it will not get too brown. When done, top should be smooth and a rich brown and a skewer pushed in the centre should come out clean. Allow cake to stand in tin until cool, then turn it out carefully onto a wire tray. Allow it to stand overnight to get quite cold then store in tin and keep for three weeks before icing.

ALMOND PASTE

Make as for Simnel cake, see page 138, using half quantity of ingredients.

ROYAL ICING

1½ lb. icing sugar
3–4 egg whites
1 tablespoon lemon juice

Sieve sugar into mixing bowl. Beat 3 egg whites until fluffy. Add egg whites gradually to the icing sugar, then add strained lemon juice. Beat 5–10 minutes until very white and smooth. If the eggs are small, a fourth egg white may be necessary, but do not get the icing too thin. The icing should form small peaks when lifted on the point of a knife. Use at once or keep covered with a damp cloth to prevent it hardening on top.

TO APPLY ALMOND PASTE

Brush a coating of melted and sieved apricot jam or golden syrup over the top and sides of the cake. Roll out half the almond paste in a round about ¼-inch thick to fit top of the cake. Invert cake on top of the round of paste and with a knife press almond paste inwards so that it fits neatly. Turn cake right way up and run a rolling pin lightly across the top to make sure the paste is firmly fixed. Roll out remaining paste into a strip as near as possible the width of the side of the cake and long enough to go round the cake.

Measure with a string round cake to get correct length for the almond paste. Trim edges of almond paste strip and put it round side of the cake,

pressing all joins together. Then roll a small jam jar all round the outside of the paste to get a smooth finish. Leave overnight in a cold place before applying the Royal icing.

TO APPLY ROYAL ICING

Place the cake on an icing turntable or inverted soup plate. Cover cake all over with a thin layer of Royal icing. Leave this to set, then pour on the remaining icing on top of the cake allowing it to spread and run down the sides. With the end of palette knife pat icing all over quickly, lifting it up in peaks. These will set almost at once. Apply the decorations before icing is set quite hard.

LEMON CURD TARTS

(Illustrated in colour on page 143)

Preparation time 20–25 minutes
Cooking time 12–15 minutes
To make 12 tarts

You will need

4 oz. butter
2 oz. icing sugar, sieved
7 oz. plain flour
1 oz. cornflour
¼ teaspoon salt
yolk 1 large egg, beaten
about 1 tablespoon milk
4–6 oz. lemon curd, see page 110

Soften butter and cream it with sugar until light. Sieve flour, cornflour and salt together and work this into creamed mixture. Add egg yolk until a firm dough is formed. Add a little milk only if dough is too crumbly. Dust small non–stick aluminium tartlet tins with flour. Roll out pastry thinly and cut into rounds with a fluted cutter a little larger than tops of the tart tins. Press firmly into the tins. Add ½ teaspoon lemon curd and bake in middle of moderately hot oven (400°F. or Gas Mark 6), 12–15 minutes.

Note

Lemon curd is apt to boil up when cooking and overflow the tart tins, so it is a good idea to put only a little of the curd in the tarts when filling *before*, baking, and *after* they are baked and hot from the oven, add a little extra curd. This will melt and spread over the tarts and gives much neater, well filled tarts.

SIMNEL CAKE

Preparation time 40 minutes
Cooking time 2½–2¾ hours

You will need

6 oz. butter *or* margarine
6 oz. soft brown sugar
3 eggs
6 oz. plain flour, sieved
3 rounded teaspoons mixed spice
2 oz. almonds, chopped
6 oz. currants
4 oz. sultanas
2 oz. glacé cherries, chopped
2 oz. mixed cut peel

ALMOND PASTE

1 lb. ground almonds
8 oz. castor sugar
6 oz. icing sugar, sieved
2 eggs
1 tablespoon apricot jam
1 lb. almond paste

DECORATION

1 dessertspoon cocoa powder
few drops red colouring
2 Easter chicks
coconut, finely shredded
3 small Easter egg sweets
2 lengths yellow ribbon
sprig of mimosa

Cream the butter or margarine and sugar together until light and fluffy. Beat in the eggs, one at a time, adding a little of the sieved flour with every egg after the first. Fold in remaining sieved flour and spice. Finally fold in the almonds, fruit and peel. Place half the mixture in a 7-inch round cake tin, previously lined with a double thickness of greaseproof paper and brushed all round inside with melted fat. Tie several thicknesses of brown paper or foil round the cake tin to come 1½-inches above the rim. Stand cake tin on a pad of paper on a baking sheet. Smooth the top over evenly.

TO MAKE ALMOND PASTE

Mix almonds and sugar together. Add beaten egg gradually. Knead with hands until smooth. Roll out half almond paste on a board dusted with icing sugar, into a 7-inch round. Place on top

Simnel cake

of cake mixture in tin. Place remaining cake mixture on top and smooth over. Bake in a pre-heated slow oven (310°F. or Gas Mark 2), on the middle shelf of 2½–2¾ hours. Leave in the tin for 3–5 minutes, turn out and cool on a wire tray.

TO DECORATE THE CAKE

Brush the top edge of the cake with apricot jam. Roll out a third of remaining paste to a 7-inch round and place on top of the cake. Roll out half the remaining paste into a roll to fit around the edge of the cake. Press down all round with a fork to give a ridged effect. Roll out half the remaining almond paste into eleven small round balls. Toss each one of the balls in cocoa powder and place around the inside edge of the cake. Colour the remaining almond paste red, roll out and cut out a circle with a 2-inch plain cutter. Place in the centre of the cake. Decorate with small chicks and a 'bird's nest' made from shredded coconut and filled with small Easter egg sweets. Tie ribbons round edge of the cake.

SCOTCH SHORTBREAD

Preparation time 20 minutes
Cooking time 35–40 minutes

You will need

6 oz. plain flour
4 oz. butter *or* margarine
2 oz. castor sugar

Sieve the flour into a mixing bowl. Add the butter or margarine and sugar and rub in with the fingertips. Knead on a board until a smooth dough is obtained. Press the shortbread dough into a fluted flan ring, placed on a baking sheet. Prick with a fork. Bake on middle shelf of a very moderate oven (335°F. or Gas Mark 3), for 35–40 minutes. Remove and cool on wire tray. Sprinkle with castor sugar.

If liked, the shortbread can be cut into triangles, known as 'petticoat tails'.

CHOCOLATE CAKE

Preparation time 15–20 minutes
Cooking time 1–1¼ hours

You will need

6 oz. self-raising flour
2 oz. sweetened chocolate powder
pinch salt
2 eggs
4 oz. butter
4 oz. sugar
1 tablespoon golden syrup
milk to mix, if necessary
castor sugar, to sprinkle

Grease and line a 7-inch cake tin. Sieve flour, chocolate powder and salt together. Beat eggs well.

Chocolate cake

Cream butter and sugar. Add eggs and dry ingredients alternately to the creamed mixture, beating well. After all flour is added, add the melted syrup and milk, if necessary, to make a softly dropping consistency. Pour into the tin, smoothing the top. Bake in middle of a moderately hot oven (400°F. or Gas Mark 6), 1–1¼ hours. Cool slightly in tin before turning out onto wire tray.

SEED CAKE (ENGLISH MIDLANDS)

Preparation time 20 minutes
Cooking time 1¼–1½ hours

You will need

1 oz. caraway seeds
10 oz. plain flour
1 teaspoon baking powder
pinch salt
4 oz. butter
4 oz. castor sugar
1 egg
2–3 tablespoons milk
sugar, to sprinkle

Crush the seeds with rolling pin to bring out the flavour. Sieve flour, baking powder and salt together, rub in the fat, add sugar and caraway seeds. Mix with beaten egg and a little milk, then add milk to make a softly dropping consistency. Put mixture into greased 1 lb. loaf tin. Sprinkle top with sugar and bake in moderate oven (350°F. or Gas Mark 4) for 1¼–1½ hours.

ECCLES CAKES

Roll out 6 oz. flaky pastry, see page 77, thinly, then cut into rounds with a 4-inch cutter. Mix 3 oz. currants, 1 oz. chopped candied peel, ¼ teaspoon grated nutmeg, 1½ oz. granulated sugar and 1 oz. melted butter and put a teaspoon of the mixture in centre of each. Dampen edges of pastry and gather together in centre, forming a round. Turn over and press lightly with rolling pin. Snip in centre with scissors. Brush with water and sprinkle with sugar. Bake in hot oven (425°F. or Gas Mark 7), for 15–20 minutes.

GLOUCESTER GINGERBREAD

Preparation time 20–25 minutes
Cooking time 1¼–1½ hours

You will need

4 oz. butter
6 oz. black treacle
2 oz. golden syrup
¼ pint (U.S. ⅝ cup) milk
2 eggs
10 oz. plain flour
2 oz. brown sugar
1 rounded teaspoon mixed spice
1 level teaspoon bicarbonate of soda
2 level teaspoons ground ginger

Using a large saucepan, warm together butter, treacle and syrup. Add milk and allow mixture to cool. Beat eggs and add to cooled mixture. Sieve dry ingredients together in a bowl, add the cooled mixture and blend in with a tablespoon. Turn into a greased and lined 7-inch square cake tin. Bake on the middle shelf of a slow oven (310°F. or Gas Mark 2), for 1¼–1½ hours.

MARBLE CAKE

(Illustrated in colour on page 143)
Preparation time 20–25 minutes
Cooking time 1¼–1½ hours

You will need

8 oz. butter
8 oz. castor sugar
3 eggs
12 oz. self-raising flour
2–3 tablespoons milk
½ teaspoon vanilla essence
2 rounded tablespoons sweetened chocolate
    powder

GLACÉ ICING

6 oz. icing sugar, sieved
2 tablespoons tepid water

Have ready an oiled and floured ring mould 9–10-inches across and 2–2½-inches deep. Soften butter in large mixing bowl, cream butter and sugar until light. Beat eggs; sieve flour. Add a little egg to the creamed mixture and beat well, then add remaining egg alternately with about

1 tablespoon of the flour; beat well with each addition. When all the egg has been added beat the mixture for 2–3 minutes. Add 2 tablespoons milk, then fold in remaining flour, adding the essence last. The mixture should be the consistency of thick batter, if too stiff add remaining tablespoon of milk.

Put about one third of mixture into another basin and add the chocolate powder, mixing it lightly but well.

To get the marbled effect of the cake, put a layer of the light coloured mixture in the prepared ring mould. On top of this drop spoonsful of the chocolate mixture, then with a knife cut through the mixture so that the chocolate runs into the light mixture. Repeat these two layers; always use less of the chocolate mixture than the light coloured mixture. The ring mould should be three quarters full. Bake in middle of a moderate oven (350°F. or Gas Mark 4), for 1½ hours. The cake should be well risen and spongy to the touch when done. Allow to cool in tin until cake shrinks from sides, then invert tin onto a large plate and shake gently to turn out. Leave to go quite cold before icing.

TO MAKE THE GLACÉ ICING

Put sugar in a bowl and add water gradually until the icing coats the back of the spoon and settles smoothly into that in the basin. Stir well; do not beat. The best way to apply this icing is to pour it round top of cake and let it settle and run down the sides.

'One stage' Victoria sandwich

BANBURY CAKES

Preparation time 25–30 minutes
Cooking time 25 minutes
To make 6 cakes

You will need

6 oz. flaky pastry, see page 77

FILLING

1 oz. butter
1 oz. brown sugar
1 oz. breadcrumbs or cake crumbs
4 oz. currants
1 tablespoon brandy

1 egg white
sugar, to sprinkle

Roll pastry out to ¼-inch thick, and cut into rounds using a small saucer for guide. Melt butter and mix all the filling ingredients together. Put in centre of rounds. Wet edges of pastry and gather them together in the middle, pressing firmly. Turn over, and press lightly into oval shape.
Slash across, brush with egg white and sprinkle with sugar. Bake in hot oven (425°F. or Gas Mark 7), 20–25 minutes.

'ONE STAGE' VICTORIA SANDWICH

Preparation time 4–5 minutes
Cooking time 25–30 minutes

You will need

6 oz. softened butter *or* luxury margarine
6 oz. castor sugar
3 eggs
6 oz. self-raising flour

Place all ingredients in a warm bowl and beat together, with a wooden spoon until well mixed, 2–3 minutes. Divide between two 7-inch greased sandwich tins. Bake on the middle shelf of a very moderate oven (335°F. or Gas Mark 3) for 25–30 minutes.
Turn out and cool on a wire tray. When cool, sandwich together with jam or cream and sprinkle the top with icing or castor sugar.

Brandy snaps

BRANDY SNAPS

Preparation time 15 minutes
Cooking time 15–20 minutes
To make 16–18

You will need

2 tablespoons treacle
2 oz. butter
2 oz. castor sugar
2 oz. flour
½ teaspoon ground ginger
1 teaspoon brandy
¼ pint (U.S. ⅝ cup) double cream, whipped

Melt treacle, butter and sugar in a pan. Mix flour and ginger and add to melted ingredients, away from heat. Lastly add the brandy. Drop in teaspoons on greased baking sheet, 4–5-inches apart. Bake in moderate oven (350°F. or Gas Mark 4), for 8–10 minutes. Allow to cool for a few seconds then remove them with a palette knife and curl round the greased handle of a wooden spoon.
When cool fill with whipped cream.

Note

Keep the brandy snaps warm until the rolling is done, as it is impossible to do this if they become too cool.
It is essential to work quickly until all the brandy snaps have been rolled.

EVERYDAY FRUIT CAKE

(Illustrated in colour on opposite page)

Preparation time 20–25 minutes
Cooking time 1½–1¾ hours

You will need

1 lb. self-raising flour
¼ teaspoon salt
½ teaspoon cream of tartar
1 teaspoon bicarbonate of soda
6 oz. butter
6 oz. castor sugar
1 lb. mixed dried fruit, including chopped
    candied peel
3 eggs
¼ pint (U.S. ⅝ cup) milk
½ teaspoon vanilla essence

Grease and paper line an oblong loaf tin, 9-inches
by 5-inches, and allow the paper to extend a little
way above sides of tin. Grease paper on the inner
side next to the cake.
Sieve flour and salt, cream of tartar and bicarbonate
of soda into a mixing bowl, and mix well. Rub in
fat. Add sugar and mixed fruit and stir until
thoroughly blended. Beat eggs lightly, just sufficient
to mix the yolks and whites. Add eggs gradually
to the dry mixture, blending well before adding
sufficient milk to make a stiffly dropping consistency.
It is best to use a large metal spoon for this mixing.
Add the vanilla essence last of all.
Turn mixture into prepared cake tin, spreading it
evenly. Bake in a moderately hot (375°F. or Gas
Mark 5), for the first 15 minutes, then reduce heat
to (350°F. or Gas Mark 4) and bake for a further
1½–1¾ hours, covering top with paper when cake
begins to brown, to prevent over browning. The
cake should be evenly brown and firm to the touch
when done; a shallow crack down the middle is
characteristic of this cake.

CHERRY TEA BREAD

(Illustrated in colour on opposite page)

Preparation time 15–20 minutes
Cooking time 35–40 minutes

You will need

8 oz. self-raising flour
good pinch salt
2 oz. castor sugar
3 oz. glacé cherries
¼ pint (U.S. ⅝ cup) milk
1 large egg
2 tablespoons melted butter

Grease and flour an ovenproof dish or straight
sided 8-inch aluminium cake tin.
Pre-heat oven to (375°F. or Gas Mark 5).
Sieve flour, salt and sugar into mixing bowl. Chop
2 oz. of the cherries into quarters; toss in flour to
dry them and then add to mixture in bowl. Beat egg
and mix it with half the milk. Stir this gradually
into dry mixture. Add the melted butter and more
milk if necessary to make a stiffly dropping consistency. Put mixture into prepared dish or tin, three
quarters filling it, and spread it evenly. Cut remaining cherries into halves and arrange them on top
of the cake. Put cake on middle shelf of oven, and
reduce heat to (350°F. or Gas Mark 4), and bake
for 35–40 minutes or until a good golden brown
and firm to the touch.
Leave to cool in the dish or tin.

Note

There may be a little more mixture than is required
for the cake.
If so, it can be used for buns, each one topped
with ½ a cherry.
Bake these for 12–15 minutes.

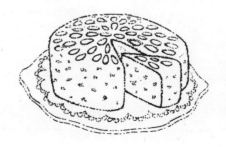

Marble cake; everyday fruit cake; cherry tea bread; Scotch pancakes; lemon curd tarts

1 Stilton stuffed tomatoes

2—6 A selection of cheeses

7 Cheese nut balls

CHEESE AND HOME-MADE WINES

CHEESE

A whole book could be written about the cheeses of the British Isles, their history and tradition and the folk lore attached to them, for each one has its own story. The flavour of our cheeses varies according to the district in which it is made.

CHEDDAR is perhaps the most popular.
It has been a favourite since Tudor times and has firm composition and a sharp tang. Being so firm it is excellent for cooked cheese dishes.

CHESHIRE CHEESE is one of the oldest English cheeses. It is a curdy, rather crumbly cheese with a superb tangy flavour. As it matures it takes on a rosy apricot tint. Blue Cheshire is so called because of the blue veins that run through it. There is also a Red Cheshire much favoured in the North.

LANCASHIRE CHEESE is a very similar cheese to the Cheshire, but somewhat harder. Lancashire cheese is excellent for cooking.

LEICESTER CHEESE is another hard cheese, made from whole milk, and somewhat like the Cheddar. It is made in the shape of a flat millstone. It has a milk flavour, is excellent for grating to use in cheese dishes.

WENSLEYDALE CHEESE certainly is the most subtly flavoured of all cheeses with an after-taste that can only be described as honey like.

STILTON CHEESE is considered the aristocrat of English chesses. It is a double cream, blue moulded semi-hard cheese, when fully ripe it is creamy white with veins of blue mould evenly distributed throughout. The rind is always crinkly, but it should not be cracked. There is a lot of controversy about the correct way to serve Stilton. It was traditional to scoop it out from the centre with a long spoon specially made for the purpose, but this method is now considered wasteful since it leaves a crumbly outer rim that dries up. Now it is recommended that the cheese be cut straight across in slices and that it be covered with a cloth to keep it moist. Nor should port wine ever be poured into it.

DOUBLE GLOUCESTER was Charles Lamb's favourite; the prefix 'double' refers to its size. There used to be a single Gloucester, half as big.

DERBY is creamy white with clean, mild flavour, texture smooth and close. SAGE DERBY is flavoured with sage leaves, and has layers of pale green in it.

CAERPHILLY, named after the Glamorgan village where it was first made, has a gentle mildly lactic tang; it is moist, but firm with a very thin rind, a full cream cheese.
There are several local cheeses that seldom leave their own district; the BLUE DORSET, or BLUE VINNY, Oxfordshire cheese; SLIPCOTE, made in Rutland; DUNLOP, a Scottish cheese, and many makes of cream and curd cheese, those from Devon and Cornwall being regarded as the best. YORK and CAMBRIDGE cheese are soft and as good as some of the Continental cheese of the same type.

CHEESE AND NUT BALLS

(Illustrated in colour on page 144)

Preparation time 20–30 minutes
Cooking time no cooking
To serve 2–3

You will need

8 oz. cream cheese
2 oz. fine white breadcrumbs
2 oz. chopped toasted almonds
salt and pepper

Press the cream cheese with a fork, add the breadcrumbs, mix well then add most of the chopped toasted almonds. Season to taste with salt and pepper. Chill until firm. Shape into balls with fingers dipped in flour, then roll the balls on a board sprinkled with the remaining chopped almonds. Place on cocktail sticks and chill well before serving.

YORKSHIRE CURD CHEESE TART

(Illustrated in colour on page 85)

Preparation time 20–30 minutes
Cooking time 25–30 minutes
To serve 4–5

You will need

6 oz. short pastry, see page 77
1 oz. butter
1 oz. castor sugar
8 oz. curd *or* cream cheese
1 egg
½ oz. sultanas
¼ oz. currants
¼ oz. finely chopped peel
grated rind ½ lemon
pinch salt
grated nutmeg
2 tablespoons milk
1 tablespoon thin cream

Line a straight sided tart tin, 6–7-inches with the pastry, pressing it well down on base of tin and round the sides. Prick bottom of pastry, and press

again with backs of fingers so that all air is expelled and holes are sealed so that the filling cannot run under the pastry and cause it to rise in the tin. With back of forefinger press the pastry into the angle where side of tin joins bottom. Mark the edges of pastry with a fork. This helps to secure the pastry to the rim of the the tin as well as giving a pretty finish.

TO MAKE THE CURD FILLING

Soften butter; cream butter and sugar together, work into the curds, add beaten egg and mix until quite smooth. Add fruit, grated lemon rind, juice, grated nutmeg and pinch of salt, mix well, then add milk and cream. The mixture should be the consistency of thick cream. Pour into pastry lined tin, grate a little nutmeg over the top. Bake in a moderately hot oven (375 °F. or Gas Mark 5), for 30 minutes, until curd is set and a good golden brown on top.

Note

Some old recipes say that 1 teaspoon brandy may be added to the curd filling.

STILTON STUFFED TOMATOES

(Illustrated in colour on page 144)

Preparation time 30–40 minutes
Cooking time no cooking
To serve 4

You will need

6 firm, medium-sized tomatoes
4 oz. Stilton cheese
1 oz. butter
2 teaspoons finely chopped chives
  or green tops of spring onions
pinch cayenne pepper

Wipe the tomatoes, cut a ½-inch slice from the stalk end. Make a pointed edge to the tomatoes by removing small triangles of the flesh with a sharp pointed knife. Then cut out some of the pulp of the tomatoes. Sprinkle inside the tomatoes with a little salt and pepper. Crumble the cheese with a fork, work in the butter, the finely chopped chives or spring onions, season with cayenne pepper. Chill well, then pile the cheese mixture into the tomato cases.

HOME-MADE WINES AND OTHER DRINKS

The quantity of liquid used in these recipes gives the yield.

DANDELION WINE Wash 6 pints (U.S. 15 cups) flower heads, put in bowl, cover with 1 gallon (U.S. 20 cups) boiling water, leave for 3 days, stirring every day. Squeeze flowers out, put liquid in pan with the rind and juice of 1 orange and lemon, 1 lb. sugar and 1-inch bruised root ginger, and boil for 30 minutes. Pour out and leave to cool, then add 1 oz. yeast on a slice of toast. Leave to ferment for 6 days, then strain into jar or cask, bunging lightly until fermentation ceases, then tighten bung and leave for 6 months. Bottle off, cork tightly and leave another 3 months.

ELDERBERRY WINE Strip stalks from 4 lb. berries. Boil in 1 gallon (U.S. 20 cups) water for 10 minutes. Strain, add 3 lb. sugar to liquid with 8 oz. chopped raisins ad simmer 20 minutes. Let it cool in bowl then add 1 oz. yeast spread on toast, leave to ferment 3 weeks, then skim and strain into a stone jar. Leave open until fermentation ceases, then bung tightly. Leave for 6 months, then bottle. Cork tightly and leave at least 3 months.

BLACKBERRY WINE Pour 1 gallon (U.S. 20 cups) boiling water over 2 lb. blackberries and 8 oz. well pricked damsons, leave for a week, stirring each day, pressing the fruit well. Strain, add 3 lb. sugar and mix well, then add ½ oz. yeast spread on toast.
Cover lightly and leave for 10–14 days, skim and strain through muslin placed in funnel into stone jar or cask; bung loosely, leave until froth subsides, then see that the jar is filled to the brim and bung tightly. Draw off into bottles after 6 months, cork tightly and keep another 3 months.

PARSNIP WINE Peel and wash 5 lb. young parsnips, cut them up and boil in 1 gallon (U.S. 20 cups) water until tender. Stir and press well, then strain through a jelly bag. Add 4 lb. sugar and 1 oz. bruised root ginger and boil until sugar has dissolved. Pour into a bowl and add juice and rind of 1 lemon (yellow part only) and 4 oz.

chopped raisins. Cool and add 1 oz. yeast spread on toast. Cover with muslin and leave for 14 days removing scum as it rises. Then strain into cask or jar. Bung or cork tightly when fermentation ceases, leave for 6 months, then bottle off and leave for another 3 months.

DAMSON WINE Wipe and prick 4 lb. damsons, and pour 1 gallon (U.S. 20 cups) boiling water over. Add ½ oz. stick cinnamon, cover and leave for 4 days stirring every day, crushing fruit. Strain and add 4 lb. sugar and stir until dissolved. Then strain again through flannel or filter paper, add 1 oz. yeast on toast and leave to ferment for 14 days. Skim and pour into cask or jar, bung lightly until frothing ceases, then bung tightly. Leave for 6 months, then bottle. Cork tightly and leave at least 3 months.

MULLED ALE Put 2 pints (U.S. 5 cups) ale or light beer, 6 cloves, piece root ginger, ¼ nutmeg, 1 dessertspoon honey or brown sugar in a saucepan, bring to boiling point and simmer, do not let it actually boil, for 3–4 minutes. Strain, add 2 tablespoons rum or brandy and serve at once.

GINGER BEER Pare off the yellow part of the rind of 2 lemons and squeeze juice into a bowl, add 1½ lb. sugar, 1 oz. bruised root ginger and ½ oz. cream of tartar. Pour 6 pints (U.S. 15 cups) boiling water over. When lukewarm add 1 oz. yeast, creamed with a little of the beer and spread on a slice of toast. Ferment for 24 hours then strain and bottle and tie down securely.

PUNCH Rub the rinds of 1 lemon and 1 Seville orange, or an ordinary orange if Sevilles are out of season, with lump sugar, until the yellow part is rubbed off. Put in a punch bowl with more sugar to make up to 4 oz. Strain over the sugar the juice of the fruit, add 6 cloves and ½ nutmeg, grated. Pour over these 1 pint (U.S. 2½ cups) boiling water and stir until sugar dissolves. Add ¼ pint (U.S. ⅝ cup) rum and ⅓ pint (U.S. ⅝ cup) brandy, stir well, cover with cloth or lid for a few minutes and serve hot.
For a more potent brew use claret or other light red wine instead of water.

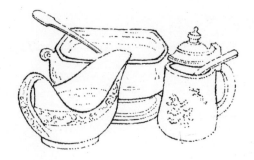

SAUCES FOR REFERENCE

'One can learn to cook, and one can be taught to roast, but a good sauce maker is a genius, born, not made' (Brillat-Savarin). But since genius is 'an infinite capacity for taking pains', there is no real reason why every cook should not be a good sauce maker.

People who 'can't be bothered to make sauce', say that sauces are used to cover up bad cooking or disguise inferior meats or fish. This should never be the case. A sauce should be a good thing on its own, and while it can add richness to a meal, its flavour should never 'kill' the natural flavour of the food it accompanies.

FOUNDATION WHITE SAUCE

Preparation time	4 minutes
Cooking time	4 minutes
To serve	4

You will need

2 oz. butter
2 oz. flour, sieved
½ pint (U.S. 1¼ cups) milk
½ pint (U.S. 1¼ cups) meat *or* vegetable stock, fish stock for fish
salt and pepper

Melt the butter, stir in the flour gradually, away from the heat, until a smooth paste is formed. Add warmed milk and stock, beating well. Stir over low heat until boiling, simmer gently, stirring often for 4–5 minutes.

VARIATIONS

RICH WHITE SAUCE — add 1 tablespoon of cream at the end. Serve plain with vegetables, boiled or steamed fish and poultry, boiled meats.

CAPER SAUCE — add 1 tablespoon capers to ½ pint (U.S. 1¼ cups) white sauce. Use with boiled mutton. Also good with fish.

PARSLEY SAUCE — add 1 dessertspoon finely chopped parsley to ½ pint (U.S. 1¼ cups) white sauce. For extra good flavour, simmer the stalks of the parsley in ½ pint (U.S. 1¼ cups) water before making white sauce. If sauce is to be used with fish, fish stock or liquor from steamed or boiled fish could be used. Serve with boiled fish, particularly cod, and broad beans.

CHEESE SAUCE — add 2 oz. grated cheese to ½ pint (U.S. 1¼ cups) white sauce; stir well until cheese melts. Use for au gratin dishes, e.g. cauliflower, leeks, celery, flaked boned fish, macaroni cheese, where the sauce is poured over the cooked food, sprinkled with grated cheese and breadcrumbs and browned under the grill.

EGG SAUCE — add 1 chopped hard-boiled egg to ½ pint (U.S. 1¼ cups) white sauce. Serve with fish or vegetables.

ONION SAUCE — add 2 large onions, boiled, drained and chopped, to ½ pint (U.S. 1¼ cups) white sauce. The water from boiling the onions should be used for making the white sauce. Usually served with boiled mutton, but is equally good with boiled fowl and boiled beef.

MUSTARD SAUCE — add 1 teaspoon dry mustard and 1 teaspoon vinegar to ½ pint (U.S. 1¼ cups) white sauce; do not reboil after adding vinegar. Serve with fish, roast or boiled pork and bacon.

CELERY SAUCE — add 12 oz. boiled and sieved celery to ½ pint (U.S. 1¼ cups) rich white sauce; use celery water when mixing sauce. Use for boiled turkey and fowls.

WATERCRESS SAUCE — add 1 dessertspoon finely chopped watercress to ½ pint (U.S. 1¼ cups) white sauce. As with parsley sauce, boil the stalks of watercress to use when making white sauce. A natural accompaniment to freshwater fish, but can be used with all boiled or steamed fish.

SORREL SAUCE — add 1 tablespoon finely chopped fresh sorrel leaves to ½ pint (U.S. 1¼ cups) rich white sauce, together with a grating of nutmeg. This old fashioned English sauce, with a slightly acid taste, from the wild sorrel leaves, was served with roast goose.

MUSHROOM SAUCE — add 2 oz. chopped and sautéed mushrooms to ½ pint (U.S. 1¼ cups) rich white sauce. To sauté mushrooms, skin and chop them and toss in butter over low heat for 8–10 minutes. Make the sauce thoroughly hot before serving. Serve with grilled meat and fish.

ANCHOVY SAUCE — add 2 desalted anchovies that have been pounded and rubbed through a sieve to ½ pint (U.S. 1¼ cups) rich white sauce. A quicker way is to add 1–2 teaspoons, according to taste of anchovy essence to ½ pint (U.S. 1¼ cups) sauce, but the flavour is not so good. Serve with fish.

FOUNDATION BROWN SAUCE

Preparation time	20 minutes
Cooking time	20 minutes
To serve	4–6

You will need

2 oz. dripping
1 medium-sized onion
3 oz. browned flour
1 pint (U.S. 2½ cups) stock
1 small carrot
1 piece of turnip
pinch mixed herbs
salt and pepper

Melt the dripping, chop onion and fry slightly. Add flour and stir until smooth and lightly browned. Stir in stock, away from heat, until mixture is free from lumps. Add chopped vegetables, herbs and seasonings and simmer 30 minutes, then strain.

VARIATIONS

RICH BROWN SAUCE — use butter instead of dripping and fry a slice of bacon or ham along with the vegetables which should include 1 or 2 chopped mushrooms and a tomato. At the end add 1–2 tablespoons sherry or Madeira. Serve with croquettes, rissoles, grilled meat and fish.

BROWN CAPER SAUCE — add 1 tablespoon chopped capers, 1 tablespoon vinegar, 1 teaspoon anchovy essence to ½ pint (U.S. 1¼ cups) brown, sauce. Serve with grilled meats, liver, kidneys, and grilled fish.

BROWN ONION SAUCE — add 2 chopped and sautéed onions to ½ pint (U.S. 1¼ cups) rich brown sauce. Sauté onions in butter. Serve with roast mutton.

HAM SAUCE — add 2 tablespoons chopped cooked ham, 1 dessertspoon chopped parsley, a squeeze lemon juice to ½ pint (U.S. 1¼ cups) brown sauce. Serve with veal and duck.

OLIVE SAUCE — add 1 dozen chopped stuffed olives to ½ pint (U.S. 1¼ cups) brown sauce. Simmer olives in sauce for 15 minutes, and add a squeeze lemon juice just before serving. Serve with roast veal and poultry.

MAYONNAISE SAUCE

Preparation time	10 minutes
Cooking time	10 minutes
To serve	4

You will need

1 teaspoon dry mustard
salt and pepper
¼ teaspoon castor sugar
1 egg yolk
¼ pint (U.S. ⅝ cup) olive oil
1 teaspoon tarragon vinegar
1 teaspoon white vinegar
1 tablespoon thin cream *or* top milk

Mix together the mustard, salt and pepper, add sugar. Stir in the beaten egg yolk. Whisk in the olive oil drop by drop. As the mixture thickens add the vinegar. Lastly add the cream or top milk slowly, stirring gently until well blended.

VARIATION

TARTARE SAUCE — add 1 tablespoon chopped gherkins or capers and 1 teaspoon chopped parsley to ½ pint (U.S. 1¼ cups) mayonnaise sauce. Serve with fish.

BREAD SAUCE

Preparation time 10 minutes
Cooking time 30–35 minutes
To serve 4

You will need

½ pint (U.S. 1¼ cups) milk
1 onion stuck with a clove
1 blade mace
2 oz. soft, white breadcrumbs
salt and pepper
1 oz. butter *or* margarine
1 dessertspoon thin cream

Heat the milk in double boiler, with the onion and clove and blade of mace. Bring to boiling point, keep at this point for 20 minutes. Remove onion and mace. Sprinkle in breadcrumbs, beating well, add salt and pepper to taste and half the butter or margarine. Bring to boiling point, beating all the time. Remove from heat and add cream and rest of butter, blending well. Serve with roast chicken and turkey.

DEVIL SAUCE

Preparation time 20 minutes
Cooking time 20 minutes, including brown sauce
To serve 4

You will need

1 dessertspoon granulated sugar
3 tablespoons foundation brown sauce, see page 148
3 oz. melted butter
juice 1 lemon
1 tablespoon Worcestershire sauce
1 tablespoon white wine *or* dry cider
1 teaspoon cayenne pepper

Dissolve the sugar in the brown sauce, then add the rest of the ingredients, mix well together and make thoroughly hot. Serve with devilled turkey legs, game, kidneys.

CUMBERLAND SAUCE

Preparation time 8–10 minutes
Cooking time 10–15 minutes
To serve 4

You will need

1 large orange
1 lemon
$^1/_8$ pint (U.S. scant $^5/_8$ cup) water
2 tablespoons port wine
2 tablespoons vinegar
2 tablespoons red currant jelly
¼ teaspoon mixed mustard
good pinch salt
dash cayenne pepper
6 glacé cherries *or* cranberries, chopped

Grate yellow rinds of orange and lemon; add to water and simmer 5 minutes. Add wine, vinegar, jelly, stir until jelly melts. Add orange and lemon juice, season to taste with mustard, salt and cayenne pepper, and add chopped cherries or cranberries.

OYSTER SAUCE

Open 6 oysters carefully so that all the liquor is caught. Beard and halve or quarter. Melt 1 oz. butter in saucepan, add 1 oz. flour and stir until smooth, stir in oyster liquor, pinch cayenne, little nutmeg and pinch salt. Add ½ pint (U.S. 1¼ cups) milk slowly, stir until smooth; heat over low heat, stir all the time, until creamy. Put oysters in a sieve, suspend in boiling water for a few seconds. Drain well. Put into soup tureen, pour sauce over. Serves 4.

APPLE SAUCE

Preparation time 15 minutes
Cooking time 20–25 minutes
To serve 4

You will need

1 lb. sharp apples
1 tablespoon water
2–3 cloves
1 tablespoon sugar
1 oz. butter
few drops lemon juice

Peel, quarter and core the apples. Cut into slices, place in pan with water, cloves and sugar. Simmer until tender, then remove cloves, add butter and lemon juice and beat until smooth, or rub through a sieve. Serve with roast pork and roast duck and goose.

HOLLANDAISE SAUCE

Preparation time 10 minutes
Cooking time 15 minutes
To serve 4

You will need

2 oz. butter
2 egg yolks
salt and pepper
few drops lemon juice

Melt half the butter in double saucepan, add beaten egg yolks, and stir gently until the mixture thickens. Add remainder of butter in small pieces, stirring away from heat until all is blended smoothly. Season to taste and add a few drops of lemon juice. Care should be taken that water in lower half of double saucepan does not boil too fast, or the mixture will curdle.

GAME SAUCE

Preparation time 10 minutes
Cooking time 15 minutes, after brown sauce is made
To serve 4

You will need

4 tablespoons rich brown sauce, see page 148
1 dessertspoon mushroom ketchup
1 teaspoon sugar
juice ½ lemon
¼ teaspoon cayenne pepper
⅛ teaspoon salt
1 glass port

Heat the sauce, add all the other ingredients except the port and stir over low heat until thoroughly blended. Do not allow to boil. At the last moment add port, serve immediately with roast game or duck.

RED CURRANT SAUCE

Dissolve ¼ pint (U.S $^5/_8$ cup) jar red currant jelly in 1 glass port wine in a small saucepan, over a low heat. Bring slowly to the boil; serve with jugged or roast hare and game. Serves 4.

HORSERADISH SAUCE

Blend 2 tablespoons grated horseradish, ½ teaspoon made mustard, 1 teaspoon castor sugar, and a pinch of salt and mix with 1 tablespoon white vinegar. Add ¼ pint thick cream or whipped evaporated milk slowly, beating well. Chill well before using. Serves 4.

MINT SAUCE

Preparation time 20 minutes
Cooking time no cooking
To serve 4

You will need

1 dessertspoon chopped fresh mint
1 teaspoon sugar
1 dessertspoon hot water
pinch salt
tarragon *or* wine vinegar

Mint should be young and freshly gathered. Remove leaves from stalks; wash and dry leaves in tea towel. Chop finely on a board, or use scissors. Place in small sauceboat with sugar and water. Stir until sugar dissolves. Add salt. Lastly add enough vinegar to make a thick sauce, really the mint should only be bound with the vinegar; it is wrong to serve vinegar with a few bits of mint floating in it.

WINE SAUCE

Preparation time 10 minutes
Cooking time 10 minutes
To serve 4

You will need

4 oz. loaf sugar
½ pint (U.S. 1¼ cups) water
2 tablespoons marmalade
1 glass sherry
few drops red colouring

Boil the sugar and water rapidly for 6 minutes, add the marmalade and boil a further 8 minutes. Strain, add the sherry and colouring as desired. Jam may be used instead of marmalade, but use a little less sugar and add a little lemon juice.

SWEET WHITE SAUCE

Mix 1 level dessertspoon cornflour to a smooth paste with a little of the ½ pint (U.S. 1¼ cups) milk. Put rest of milk in pan with 2–3 inches of lemon rind and 1 dessertspoon of sugar and heat until milk is well flavoured with the lemon, about 8 minutes. Do not boil. Strain milk over the blended cornflour, return all to pan and simmer 3–4 minutes. A little cream or knob of butter added at this point increases richness. Other flavourings beside lemon may be used. Serves 4.

JAM SAUCE

Boil ¼ pint (U.S. $^5/_8$ cup) water and 2 tablespoons jam for 3 minutes. Mix cornflour smoothly with a little water and add to boiling liquid. Stir until boiling. Simmer 2–3 minutes. Strain and add lemon juice or other flavouring. Serves 4.

MARMALADE SAUCE — use marmalade instead of jam, but omit the lemon juice.

CUSTARD SAUCE

Heat ½ pint (U.S. 1¼ cups) milk with a few drops vanilla essence and a pinch of salt and pour over 2 beaten egg yolks. Strain into pan, add 2 teaspoons castor sugar and stir until custard thickens, but do not let it come to the boil. Serves 4.

COFFEE SAUCE — as above using ¼ pint (U.S. $^5/_8$ cup) coffee and ¼ pint (U.S. $^5/_8$ cup) milk.

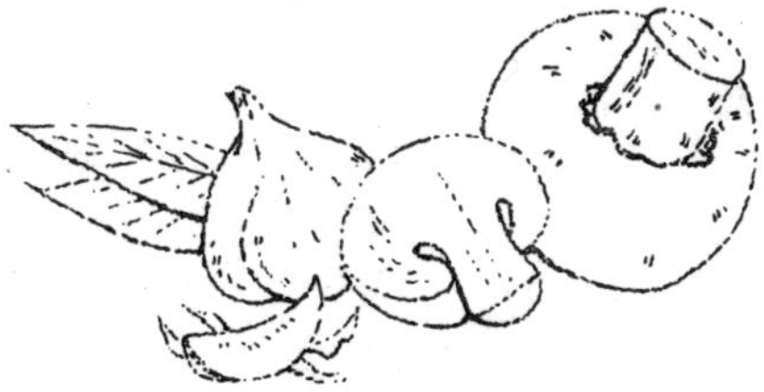

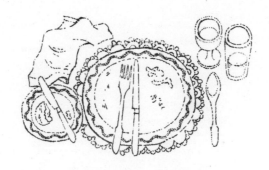

INDEX

154

ACKNOWLEDGEMENTS

The author and publishers would like to thank the following for their help in supplying photographs for this book.

Australian Recipe Service — black and white pages 22, 23.
Baco Foil Advisory Bureau — black and white page 51.
Blue Band Bureau — black and white pages 70, 90, 98, 131, 140.
British Egg Information Council — black and white pages 71, 101, 116.
British Farm Produce Council — black and white pages 23, 27.
British Travel Association — black and white page 30.
Brown and Polson — black and white pages 13, 93.
Butter Information Council — black and white pages 12, 13.
Camp Coffee — black and white page 91.
Cadbury's — black and white pages 88, 98, 139.
The Cheese Bureau — black and white page 72.
Colman's mustard — black and white pages 44, 62.
Colman's semolina — black and white page 128.
Flour Advisory Bureau — black and white pages 79, 82, 89, 129, 130 136.
Fowler's West India Treacle — black and white page 120.
Fruit Producer's Council — black and white pages 81, 111, 119.
Lard Information Bureau — black and white page 127.
Macfisheries Limited — black and white pages 41, 54.
New Zealand Lamb Information Bureau — black and white pages 26, 27, 28.
Odhams Syndication — colour frontispiece, pages 19, 20, 37, 38, 47, 48, 57, 75, 76, 85, 86, 95, 96, 114, 123, 134, 143, 144. Black and white pages 11, 14, 17, 35, 71, 72, 83, 103, 117, 131.
Outspan Fruits — colour page 113.
Polish Food Centre — black and white page 103.
Pig Industry Development Authority — black and white pages 28, 31.
Potato Marketing Board — black and white page 60.
Quaker Oats Limited — black and white page 52.
James Robertsons and Sons — black and white page 102.
Spry Cookery Service — black and white page 35.
Stork Cookery Service — colour page 124. Black and white page 138.
T. Wall and Sons (Meat and Handy Foods) Limited — black and white pages 69, 93.